CW00607324

Wooden Spoon Society

RUGBY WORLD '02

EDITED BY

Ian Robertson

Photographs by

Colorsport

Queen Anne Press

A QUEEN ANNE PRESS BOOK

First published in 2001 by
Queen Anne Press, a division of
Lennard Associates Limited
Mackerye End
Harpenden, Herts AL5 5DR

A catalogue entry is available from the British Library

ISBN 1 85291 638 9 (paperback)
ISBN 1 85291 639 7 (hardback)

Production Editor: Chris Marshall
Cover Design/Design Consultant: Paul Cooper
Reproduction: Alan Clark/Prism Digital
Printed and bound in Slovenia for Ellis Publications

The publishers would like to thank Colorsport for providing most of the
photographs for this book.

The publishers would also like to thank AllsportUK, David Gibson
(Fotosport), Leonard E Goode Photography, Inpho Sports Photography,
Terry Sellick, and Chris Thau for additional material.

The publishers would also like to thank Pat Murphy, Amy Cracknell and
Clare Robertson for their editorial assistance.

CONTENTS

If you could bank a grin, whose would it be?

 Lloyds TSB

Sponsors of the Lloyds TSB Six Nations

FOREWORD

BY **HRH THE PRINCESS ROYAL**

HRH The Princess Royal
Royal Patron
Wooden Spoon Society

BUCKINGHAM PALACE

The game of rugby has changed much over the last few years but the one constant factor in this development of the game has been the continuing growth and effectiveness of Wooden Spoon Society, the Charity of British Rugby.

Whilst much of the conversation over this time in club house and committee room has been the balance between the amateur and the professional game, members of Wooden Spoon Society bypass such fripperies and continue to raise considerable amounts of money from the compassionate side of rugby to fund Projects which benefit children and young people.

This book reflects very much the growth of the Charity and the respect that it has gained from within the game itself.

As Patron of the Society, I was able to open the Wooden Spoon Society Family Cancer Care and Haematology Unit at Stoke Mandeville in April of this year and what a wonderful unit it is. It is a unique way of approaching the treatment of cancer whereby it is a hospital without beds. The £1m invested has produced seminar and consulting rooms, treatment areas and specialists areas for analysis and dialysis whilst at the same time maintaining the ability for patients to enjoy their evenings at home rather than be hospitalised.

This modern and rather unique approach reflects Wooden Spoon itself in its own fundraising and activities.

Also this year Wooden Spoon has opened a second Wooden Spoon Society Teenage Cancer Trust Unit at Queen Elizabeth Hospital in Birmingham and a number of smaller Regional Projects. A total charitable funding of over £4.5m in the calendar year.

I am also encouraged by the continuing work of Wooden Spoon Society within the social inclusion area by developing the game of rugby for our Inner Cities.

I am pleased to support this activity and I thank you for supporting a Charity that does so much to reflect the finest team game in the world.

Anne

Wooden Spoon Society
- the Charity of British Rugby

Royal Patron: HRH The Princess Royal
Patrons: Rugby Football Union • Scottish Rugby Union
                 Welsh Rugby Union • Irish Rugby Football Union

'It's not what we do... it's what we do with the money!'

The Spoon Challenges

Canoeing down the lake with the towering mountains. Bet they didn't even notice!

Is foot-and-mouth a challenge or an affliction? It is both, and deeply do all Spoon members have compassion with all those who have suffered this year.

As the charity of British rugby, much of our revenue each year derives from rugby-related events and activities. However, the two Spoon Challenges, the Wooden Spoon Society Vauxhall Four Peaks Challenge and the Wooden Spoon Society Ford Great Lakeland Challenge, provide a major part of our annual income. We reap in excess of £500,000 each year from these two events.

When that dreadful scourge foot-and-mouth struck the nation in early spring, we all felt a deep well of sympathy for the besieged farming community. This broadened, as the disease really took hold, to the hotel and catering trade and all those who are dependent upon the free passage of people travelling about the land.

Little do people realise that we are all affected, and not least a charity like Wooden Spoon Society. Both of our Challenges are held in the very areas so badly hit and if we cannot utilise these areas then we lose our entire income.

However, undaunted we put into action some pretty swift contingency plans. We moved the Wooden Spoon Society Vauxhall Four Peaks Challenge back into September, to the last day when the daylight hours will allow us to complete the event within the 48-hour deadline. As we go to press, that event is still threatened, but we are all optimistic that we will be Four Peaking again come September.

For the Wooden Spoon Society Ford Great Lakeland Challenge we had to be a little more inventive. With only a six-week (!) lead time, our intrepid committee transferred the whole event to La Belle France and sourced a new venue in the mountains above Lake Annecy. It is a beautiful part of France and certainly no hardship to be there. However, the logistical effort required in getting there is almost a Challenge in itself and fully deserves the telling.

This particular Spoon Challenge is a very demanding form of triathlon. The three sets require teams to canoe the length of Lake Annecy (10.5 miles), then climb an equivalent peak to Scafell Pike at home (3,206 feet), and then cycle over the mountain passes of Col de Aravis for 26 miles – a pleasant day's interlude! First we had to get the teams on our side.

It is not easy to transfer such a Challenge when past performances are such a yardstick to drive on the subsequent competitors. Change the layout and the geography and you change the Challenge. Nevertheless the teams were fired up with enthusiasm and the 'never-say-die' spirit of not letting foot-and mouth-defeat us. It could also have been the attraction of visiting a most beautiful part of France!

An oasis on the climbing section of the Challenge. There was no language barrier!

Having sorted out the teams and the venue, we then needed to source the essential aspects of the Challenge – canoes (France does not seem to possess Canadian canoes, only the two-seater kayak variety) and a means of transporting our competitors' precious and in the most part very expensive cycles. Again our corporate friends stepped into the breach. Dawes Cycles plc promptly provided us with the latest in cycle protective packaging and our friends at TNT UK Express provided not one but two heavy-duty trucks to transport all the cycles and the canoes from Lakeside YMCA (our canoe sponsors) in the Lake District, UK, to Lake Annecy, France.

And what was the result of this frenetic activity… ?

£103,733.00… INCREDIBLE!!!!

Yes, that is what we raised. No, not French Francs or European Euros, but Solid Sterling.

As the teams arrived for the briefing at the remote Hostel La Ruche high up in the magnificent Col de Aravis, the rain was lashing down and few believed the prediction of sunny weather for the following day. Yet as the competitors travelled to the head of Lake Annecy the following morning, the skies cleared to bright sunshine by the start of the canoe section.

Usually the least eventful section, the canoe leg was livened up considerably by two teams who decided to cool off by practising their capsize drills en route. Both teams can now testify to the fact that Lake Annecy is the purest lake in Europe – and the wettest! The end of the leg saw Quodlibet land five minutes ahead of the field, followed by their Oxfordshire team-mates from the Moulsford Lions and In Vino Veritas.

The mountain route was tougher than many were expecting, although it did have the unexpected pleasure of gift shops and restaurants halfway up at the Col de la Forclaz! One team who weren't stopping to enjoy the view were Stragglers, who came through from eighth after the canoe leg to finish first on the mountain with an incredible display of fell running. The cycle leg saw Team Orrell Post come in to their own and they rode away from the field, finishing 25 minutes ahead of the second place team. Everyone who took part in this very unusual year deserves congratulations, but special well-dones go to: Harpooners, who defended the Challenge Bowl by completing all three sections in a time of 6 hours 34 minutes and pledged an amazing total of £9,000. Ford Fleet, who did some phenomenal fund-raising to win the Funding Bowl, pledging an enormous £12,000.

Above: It's a race, neck and neck – eventual overall winners the Harpooners pierce the delivery plans of Orrell Post. Right: Those TNT people get everywhere! Opposite, top: And for the second year, the winners are the Harpooners. Opposite, bottom: The Quodlibet quartet – all £34,004 of them!

A Special Mention

At the end of last year's event, Andy Welton of Ford Motor Company made a very generous offer, promising three months' vehicle loan to any team who returned in 2001 and brought a second team with them. Inspired by Andy's offer, Nichol and Karin Clarke pledged to return this year with four teams. True to their word they managed to find 14 willing (?!) volunteers to take up the Challenge from their spiritual base at Moulsford School in Oxfordshire. Their fund-raising was inspirational, involving much of the local community and including sponsored walks, golf days, fun auctions and a musical

evening at their local church, for which Nichol composed a special Spoon anthem. They even produced their own Wooden Spoon Society Cookery Book. All this resulted in an incredible pledge of £34,004, split evenly between the four teams. (This fact coupled with the vagaries of the Challenge scoring system narrowly denied Quodlibet the Challenge Bowl).

And you may ask again, 'What did we do with the money!?' Well in the last 12 months we have:

1. Opened the Wooden Spoon Society Teenage Cancer Trust Unit at Queen Elizabeth Hospital, Birmingham, opened by the Duchess of York (£408,000).
2. '97 Lions giant John Bentley opened our Wooden Spoon Society Sensory Room & Wooden Spoon Playground at Wasdale Respite Home for disabled children in Wakefield (£20,000).
3. John Spencer, Yorkshire rugby hero and current RFU grandee, opened the Wooden Spoon Society Living Skills Area at Welburn Hall Special School, Kirbymoorside (£100,000).
4. Our Royal Patron Her Royal Highness The Princess Royal opened Wooden Spoon

The Wooden Spooners – Halliwell Llandau.

Salute the Sponsors!

SPONSORED BY *Ford*

Besides our badging sponsors, this year we had some more friends: Centre la Ruche and the Hotel Beauregard. Thanks also to Fabienne, François and all their staff at La Scierie and particular thanks to Jerry and Kate from the Aravis Retreat. Special thanks also to Anne and Joanna Welton for making the long journey out on behalf of Ford. Andy Welton could not be with us this year, but both Anne and Joanna made admirable substitutes – and are much prettier!

House in Lambeth, South London, home of the Child Health & Development Centre (£3.1M).

5. Great comedian and Spoon supporter Frank Carson opened the Wooden Spoon Society Playground for disabled children at the Westbury Lodge Respite Home, Blackpool (£30,000).

6. Rugby giant and England legend Bill Beaumont opened Wooden Spoon House, the home of the Taunton Opportunities Group for disabled children (£232,000).

7. Media icon and rugby legend Jerry Guscott opened the Wooden Spoon Entrance Hall at Burton Hill Special School in Malmesbury.

8. That memorable England and Yorkshire wing Peter Squires opened the Wooden Spoon Specialist IT Resource Centre at Henshaws College for the Blind in Harrogate.

9. And again our Royal Patron Her Royal Highness The Princess Royal opened the Wooden Spoon Society Family Cancer Care and Haematology Unit at Stoke Mandeville Hospital (£1M).

Over £5M of capital projects in your name over the last 12 months – not a bad effort! We have many more commitments for this and coming years, not least of which is to the RFU Inner City Projects, on which we are working closely with the RFU.

Why not join us in making Wooden Spoon Society even bigger and better? Details of membership of Spoon can be had from:

Our main sponsors also raised the most money. Well done, Ford!

The Spoon Office,
35 Maugham Court,
Whitstable, Kent CT5 4RR
Tel: 01227 772295
e-mail: charity@woodenspoonsoc.org.uk
website:www.woodenspoonsoc.org.uk

passenger request: *Spoil me*

Delta BusinessElite®:

5 courses of tasty things to eat
a fine wine (or two)
all the films you've been meaning to see, TV and your kind of music
a serve yourself snack table
ice-cream sundaes so huge they're sinful

▲Delta

fly 5-Star

See your travel agent or call 0800 414 767
*Passengers with hand luggage only

delta-air.com

Wooden Spoon Society Rugby World editor and BBC rugby correspondent Ian Robertson was non-shooting captain of the Wooden Spoon team at a charity shoot at The Berkshire, sponsored by Dimon International Services, courtesy of Paul Taberer, which raised £20,000 for Wooden Spoon. The Spoon shots pictured with their captain were former rugby internationals David Trick, Jeff Probyn and Roger Uttley and racehorse trainer Ian Balding.

NEMO LIBER EST QUI CORPORI SERVIT

BY **PAUL STEPHENS**

'It hasn't all been bad, not by a long way.' No, neither Matt Dawson in reflective, repentant mood, nor Austin Healey reminding us of the only good thing he had to say about Australia. In fact it was the last line of Graham Henry's final press conference after the British & Irish Lions were obliged to reflect on their defeat in the deciding Test of a series marked by the intemperate and ill-judged outbursts of two of England's finest in their ghosted newspaper columns.

Had Henry not uttered those words, they could have come from the mouth of Francis Baron, the chief executive of the Rugby Football Union, moments after the conclusion of their Annual General Meeting at the National Exhibition Centre, the day after the Lions lost the second Test, in Melbourne. Nobody took much notice, and even fewer cared, but that afternoon in a Birmingham suburb, Brian Baister was ousted as chairman of the RFU's management board. Elected in Baister's place was Graeme Cattermole, the board's chairman of finance.

Seeking a fourth year in office, Baister came to the AGM claiming that the long-awaited agreement between the Premiership clubs and the RFU had, thanks no doubt to his negotiating skills, at last been resolved. It counted for little with the electorate, and Cattermole, with the support of Fran Cotton and seven county unions, took the vote 301-199. The core of the matter is that while there was an understanding that an agreement had been reached – as Baron confirmed during the meeting – nothing had been signed. We were not so much waiting for the ink to dry on this most consequential document, as holding our breath while the small print was pored over by the lawyers on either side.

For those of us who have watched and listened to Baister as he has evaded and avoided many of the difficult issues in three undistinguished years as chairman, this was familiar territory. Surprisingly for a former police officer, he has too often given the impression of not telling the truth, the whole truth, and nothing but the truth.

Where he has been consistent is in tolerating, if not deliberately propagating, fudge, misunderstanding and greed in the relationship between the Premiership clubs and the RFU. It remains to be seen if Cattermole can do any better. For the sake of harmony, unity of purpose, the reputation of the RFU, those who care about the game – not to mention the demands on those who play it at the highest level; and the many in the ranks below – we must pray he does.

For our prayers to be answered, we depend upon the clubs to enter into a spirit of renewal with the RFU, and in so doing put aside the extremes of wanton self-interest, the flawed philosophy which has been the principal obstacle to peace in the six years since the game embraced professionalism. So far as I know, none of the club owners believe in the Tooth Fairy any more than I do. But it will only be the few without a scintilla of cynicism in their beings who imagine that the incoming chairman's period of office will not be scarred by more of the unedifying episodes which have defaced the short life of the paid era. Maybe, just maybe, the former banker Cattermole will be welcomed by the owners and he can do business with them. The odds, though, will be long.

The game has said its goodbyes to Sir John Hall, Ashley Levett and Frank Warren, though it doesn't mean the hawks have left the sky, this troublesome trio having been replaced by Gloucester's Tom Walkinshaw, Nigel Wray at Saracens, and the outspoken Keith Barwell of Northampton, who believes the RFU are an impediment to progress for only paying the clubs a pittance. With London Scottish and Richmond having fallen by the wayside – very largely through their own financial ineptitude, by paying their players too much in awarding them overblown contracts – it is no wonder that the majority of the Premiership clubs, with a collectively appalling record of incompetent housekeeping, are losing money. But this season the RFU will pay each of the Premiership clubs not far short of £2 million. Is that a pittance when some, like Sale, are not turning over as much from their own resources in ticket sales and sponsorship?

If there is any sympathy for Baister, it is because he has been required to deal with Barwell, Wray and the intransigent Walkinshaw, especially over the issue of automatic promotion and relegation between the Premiership and National One. For the time being at least, that contentious matter has been settled, Leeds being promoted, while the unloved and unwanted Rotherham were relegated. No sooner had this been ratified than the club owners staged another piece of high-profile brinkmanship by threatening to withdraw their players from England's tour to Canada and the United States. Amid the recrimination, on an all too familiar day for the sport, the clubs cited the slow pace towards a settlement in their negotiations with the RFU. As the clubs eventually backed off and put their differences to one side, realising that they did their cause no good by using the players as pawns in this damaging dispute, Walkinshaw, the Premiership clubs' chairman, was on hand to utter some soothing words: 'We are genuinely hopeful that the progress made this week will result in a stable and long-term structure between the RFU, Premier rugby and the players.' Let us hope Cattermole isn't taken in by Walkinshaw's glib reassurance any more than he is convinced the RFU should stump up even larger sums of money for the Premiership clubs as they continue to stuff their squads with overseas players.

If the game in England is to continue to develop, it is vital that the RFU and the clubs strike a lasting accord. Walkinshaw, Wray and Barwell are seen by some on the RFU council as an unelected cabal, whose departure would be no more mourned than was Mo Mowlam's by the Ulster Unionists when she was replaced as Secretary of State for Northern Ireland. But they aren't going to go away, so Cattermole should be preparing himself for a bumpy ride.

There was even more bad news for the RFU during the summer, when it was announced that the future of Walkinshaw's Arrows Formula One racing team had been jeopardised by the withdrawal of their big-money backer Morgan Grenfell Private Equity, the investment arm of Deutsche Bank, who own 50 per cent of the team which in August was bottom of the constructors' table with just a single point, and without a race win to its name. If Walkinshaw decides the moment is right to get out of motor racing it will leave him more time to devote to rugby. Now that would make life interesting for Twickenham.

As the domestic and European campaigns pounded to a close last May, the RFU could be forgiven for believing that this was their best season since professionalism was adopted. Notwithstanding the very public spat with the England squad in November over a failure to bring an end to the nine-month-long row over players' salaries, it appeared at last as if the union were coming to terms with the demands of a game whose popularity was increasing almost as fast as the RFU's bank balance was soaring. Where

previously it had been the blazers almost to a man who failed to understand the requirements of the leading clubs, now it is increasingly apparent that it is the clubs themselves who are a greater hindrance to improvement.

Surely we are in fantasy land when we are asked to believe the club coaches and owners when they tell us there is too much rugby being played, and this is damaging to the players. Why should we when the clubs opted for the ludicrously unnecessary Zurich Championship?

The brainchild of Peter Deakin, Sale's chief executive, a man with a rugby league background, the competition featured the top eight finishers in the Premiership playing off, with a grand final at Twickenham. Never mind that we already had a well-established national knockout competition, sponsored by Tetley's, who were not at all amused at the possibility of Zurich stealing their thunder. The new tournament was flagged up as a way to decide England's championship. The winner would be allotted second place in the pecking order for the following season's Heineken European Cup.

In the glossy brochure announcing the dates and rules was the absurd declaration that the whole season would rest on one match. The Premiership winners would have to battle through the Zurich Championship before being crowned as champion club. The eight-month-long slog involving 22 league matches was, it seemed, to count for very little. Although Leicester were to emerge as winners of both Premiership and Championship, their director of rugby, the ever-pragmatic Dean Richards, dismissed the

Dorian West (left) and Austin Healey hold the Zurich Championship trophy aloft. Healey played a vital part in Leicester's treble triumph, but spoiled what had been a memorable season for him with his puerile outburst in a ghosted newspaper column while on the Lions tour in Australia.

Doctor James Robson was the busiest man on the Lions tour, and his comments about the physical demands of the absurdly long season require respect. Robson leads Scott Quinnell to the treatment room at the NorthPower Stadium during the Lions match against Australia 'A'. A destructive injury toll left the Lions underpowered for most of the tour.

hype surrounding the fledgling tournament as nonsense: 'So far as I'm concerned, and everyone at this club,' argued Richards, 'the champions of England will be the club who finish top of the Premiership.' Eventually, sanity prevailed. The Premiership hierarchy backed down and the champion club of England was the winner of the Premiership.

Play-offs have long been a part of rugby league – a game which hasn't got a lot going for it at the moment – though the last thing needed towards the end of the longest ever English union season, with a Lions tour to follow plus England's visit to North America, was another three weekends when the leading players were hauled from their armchairs to be handed an unwelcome opportunity to knock a few more lumps out of one another. By May, with the European Cup and Shield finals still to be contested, not forgetting England's game against a powerful Barbarians side, the players were not only sick of the sight of each other, but in urgent need of some rest and recuperation. No chance.

The lasting images of life with the Lions will be the scale of the injury toll and the extent of some of those problems which will only become fully apparent when the new season gets underway. For some, like the unfortunate Lawrence Dallaglio, recovery will be long, painful and slow. Graham Henry reckoned there were up to ten players in his squad requiring knee surgery.

Among the predictable welter of words in Australia, the accusations and counter-claims about key players being targeted, and the puerile rants of those who should know better, there was much wisdom in the recollections and advice of the party's senior medic, Doctor James Robson. With eight players returning home early with injury, there was no end to the medical problems. The game at large would do well to heed Robson's words; they were the most significant of the tour:

'I've been on duty almost every night,' said Robson. 'It's been bad, unfortunate and unprecedented in my experience. There are various reasons for the injuries. However, there is no doubt the season is too long and this adds to the strain. The intensity has increased by 40 per cent since the 1993 tour. You cannot regularly knock hell out of each other and expect to run around, although it is remarkable how some of these guys manage to play with the disabilities they carry from one season to the next. It is inevitable that career spans will get shorter and shorter as knee problems and arthritis set in. Something has to be done about it.'

Something was. Within days of the Lions returning from Australia, Walkinshaw and Baron were able to announce that the deal which Baister had been unable to broker had been sealed and was given an eight-year term. All that remained was for the Council of the RFU to ratify the agreement at their next meeting. This they did, with only one dissenting voice. The most important point, among several to have profound implications for the welfare of the players, was the call for the elite group to be restricted to a limit of 32 games a season.

Flagged up by Walkinshaw and Baron as an edict, the magic number is no more than a recommendation. With 22 Premiership games and ten full internationals, not to mention the European competitions, national knockout cup, the Zurich play-offs, summer tours and sevens tournaments, it is a wise, though no more than arbitrary, ceiling. Can you imagine Leicester, assuming they are in sight of the three trophies they

Francis Baron (right), the chief executive of the RFU, and Premiership clubs chairman Tom Walkinshaw make their historic announcement, proclaiming peace for our time and a limit of 32 games a season for all Premiership players.

won last season, pulling Martin Johnson out of their team because he had already reached his quota of 32 matches ahead of the decisive Premiership matches or the European Cup final? If this hypothesis appears too fantastic to comprehend, think fantasy.

Having witnessed the effect of player power in being at the forefront of the dispute over pay, which nearly led to a strike before the England v Argentina game last autumn, Matt Dawson could do his fellow players a favour by ensuring that in the board room at every Premiership club, a big poster is hung prominently to remind the owner and directors of Seneca's dictum: *Nemo Liber Est Qui Corpori Servit.* No man is free who is a slave to his body.

Don't cry for us Argentina. Rugby. moves to the front pages when the England players threaten to strike, days before the November match with the Pumas at Twickenham. Some England players were reportedly in tears after coach Clive Woodward allegedly telephoned them with threats to end their international careers.

Continued on page 3, col 8

Alison Kervin, page 40

A BRIDGE TOO FAR?: can the second-tier clubs prosper in the top flight?

BY GEOFF COOKE

The conflict that raged throughout the 2000-01 rugby season in England threatened to destroy professional rugby in its infancy. The main protagonists were the Premiership clubs and virtually the rest of the game spearheaded by the National Division One clubs, who had the keenest interest in the outcome. The RFU hovered uncertainly somewhere in between like a United Nations peacekeeping force, desperate not to upset its elite clubs who provide the international players but also conscious of its responsibilities to the rest of the game.

The battle lines were simply drawn. The Premiership clubs, struggling to extricate themselves from the financial mess they had got themselves into through apparent disregard for basic business principles, were minded to ring-fence the top division to avoid the spectre of relegation. They argued that in order to develop the professional

Mike Shelley of Leeds Tykes receives the National Division One plaque from RFU competitions chairman Jonathan Dance. Can the Tykes cut it in the big time?

game they needed a period of stability to give confidence to sponsors and potential investors and give themselves time to develop players without too much emphasis on short-term results. The second-tier clubs, also struggling to make ends meet, sometimes through overambition, protested that promotion and relegation were the lifeblood of any league competition and were adamant that they should not be denied the opportunity to rise through the ranks on merit and become one of the so-called elite.

The arguments were persuasive from both sides, and logic probably favoured the Premiership clubs. However, tradition and emotion are integral ingredients of rugby union and these proved to be powerful allies. Order was restored, and automatic promotion and relegation between the top two divisions was agreed at least until the end of the 2002-03 season.

The principle of automatic promotion and relegation in a league structure is undeniable, but at this level reality raises serious doubts about the practicality of such a principle. The gulf in core financing (from sponsorship etc) between the Premiership and the second-tier clubs is circa £1.5 million. Most National One clubs have to operate on a playing-squad budget of around £250,000. Quite apart from the obvious differential in potential salary levels the better players want to play at the highest level. In terms of recruiting talented young players, the attractions of signing for Bath as opposed to Rotherham, for example, are pretty overwhelming. The best English players are drawn to the top clubs and these clubs can also afford to attract high-quality players from other countries. The standard of play in the Premiership has consequently developed to a level of skill and intensity only just below international standard and way beyond the normal standard of play in the next league down.

So how can a National One club hope to bridge the chasm that seems to be getting wider each season? Recent history is not encouraging. West Hartlepool yo-yoed between the first and second divisions for three years and ruined themselves in the process. Since

Paul Sampson beats Doug Trivella's despairing tackle to score for Wasps against Rotherham at Loftus Road. Consistently successful in the leagues, Rotherham nevertheless found the transition to the Premiership to be beyond them.

their last relegation from the Premiership (Premiership One as was) in 1998-99, the club has gone into freefall, crashing down through the lower leagues into Division Three North (level 4), losing their ground and clubhouse on the way.

Bedford, bankrolled by boxing promoter Frank Warren, put together a good side in 1997-98 when I was director of rugby there and were promoted. However, Warren and successive owners could not maintain the financial support necessary, and after managing to survive in 1998-99, Bedford were relegated in 1999-2000 and then struggled in the second division, only just surviving, in 2000-01. They were replaced in the top flight, after a nail-biting play-off, by Rotherham, who had climbed steadily through the lower leagues, lending support to the argument that automatic promotion is essential to reward ambitious clubs. Unfortunately Rotherham were never able to come to terms with the standards of the Premiership and remained anchored at the bottom of the table throughout the season and were eventually relegated. Leeds have taken their place as the next contenders, but it remains to be seen if they will fare any better than their recent predecessors.

So is it a bridge too far? Not necessarily. There are examples of promoted clubs making the grade, notably Newcastle, who were promoted in 1996-97 and went on to win the Premiership in their first season. Northampton and Saracens have prospered, and London Irish, Bristol and Sale are other relatively recent former inhabitants of the second division.

Newcastle Falcons stepped up into Premiership One at the end of the 1996-97 season and won it at the first attempt the following year. However, they were helped by the presence of a phalanx of international stars.

But what does it take? Significant finance certainly. In the 2000-01 season the two clubs with the strongest financial backing, Leeds and Worcester, ended the season some 40 points clear of their nearest rivals, with Leeds just shading the one available promotion place. Finishing as the top club out of 14 and earning promotion is hard enough, but the problems really start once that coveted Premiership place has been achieved. Promotion does bring financial reward, particularly guaranteed core funding of around £1.5 million, but when their Premiership rivals are spending that much and more on their playing squads, the promoted club will need to generate an equivalent amount at least from other sources to get anywhere near balancing the books. Mighty Leicester, with hugely consistent success on the field and a reported turnover in excess of £7 million, are apparently only just ahead of their break-even point. How does a newly promoted club generate the additional finance necessary to survive and prosper? There is no doubt that the prospect of competing against all the top clubs and star players will boost attendances, gate receipts and takings from corporate hospitality, but if your average crowd in the second division was only 400-500, even if you quadruple attendances at increased prices, gate receipts will still only produce a small proportion of the money needed. Two thousand people paying an average of £15 at 14 home matches will only generate £420,000. Even if the promoted club manages to boost average attendance to 4,000 per match at the same price per head, gate receipts will still only produce something like 50 per cent of the cash required to meet the payroll of the playing staff, quite apart from the other expenses of running a professional operation.

Clubs must have other significant sources of revenue, and that is where a club like Worcester has a distinct advantage over all other National Division clubs and an edge on several current Premiership clubs. Worcester's excellent facilities give the club the

A view of some of the facilities on offer at Worcester RFC's Sixways headquarters.

opportunity to generate income seven days a week for 52 weeks of the year. The convenient location of the impressive Sixways complex, just off Junction 6 of the M5 motorway some 30 miles south of Birmingham, makes it an attractive venue for conferences, seminars and social functions. The club currently boasts five function suites capable of accommodating from 20 to 250 people, plus 36 corporate hospitality boxes holding 10 to 15 people on match days and doubling as small group meeting rooms during the week. These facilities are serviced by the club's own catering and conference staff and in 2000-01 hosted 800 different functions for a total of 33,464 people. On home match days there are seven well-appointed bars in operation and up to 500-600 meals are served to spectators. The 40-acre site also provides superb playing and training facilities – including four full-size pitches in addition to the main stadium pitch; five junior pitches; other grassed training areas; and a 60-metre by 30-metre indoor training area, unique in the United Kingdom. Two of the pitches have floodlights for match play and there are training lights on one other pitch. All these facilities are available for hire by other clubs and sports organisations, and Sixways is a regular training base for the England Under 19 and Under 21 squads. Worcester RFC's own playing infrastructure makes big demands on these facilities, of course, as the club runs age-group teams at every level from Under 21 down to Under 8, three ladies teams and an amateur team in the lower echelons of the league system, in addition to the professional team in National Division One. This total rugby package provides a broad base of potential income generation through the players, families, friends and supporters who use the club on a regular basis. Sunday mornings at Sixways are a sight to behold, with up to 450 youngsters and their family supporters filling the complex.

Good facilities certainly help to generate the finance necessary for a club to be able to compete in the Premiership. Those clubs promoted but immediately relegated in recent seasons – West Hartlepool, Bedford, Rotherham – did not have either the facilities or the infrastructure to compare with a club like Worcester. However, the third critical success factor is people, and a club with the best facilities and the most finance could still flounder if it does not appoint the right people in the right positions, on and off the field of play. Players are the key personnel, followed by coaching and support staff, then commercial sales and marketing people. Clubs are still driven by their on-field success, and some promoted clubs in recent seasons appear to have made the mistake of placing too much importance on the loyalty factor. They have rewarded players and coaches who have helped them to win promotion by retaining them on new contracts for their Premiership campaign, failing to appreciate the gulf in standards between the Premiership and National One. This is an emotive subject, not just with the players but also for supporters, and is a tricky management issue. As the promotion season reaches a climax, players are anxious to know if their futures are secure and can be demotivated if it is apparent that their services will not be retained should promotion be achieved. Nevertheless, the counter-argument that there can be little or no room for sentiment in business is strong, and whether the traditionalists like it or not, the fact remains that professional rugby these days is indeed a business.

There is no doubt in my mind that for a club to break into the ranks of the elite premier division of English rugby and last for more than one season at that level, it requires a huge investment in facilities, infrastructure and top-quality personnel on and off the field. The club has to have a playing budget during its promotion year that enables it to attract the best available players, so that the core of the side consists of players who can perform effectively in the Premiership the following season. This means of course that the club

Worcester's Richard Jarman spins the ball out to his back line against Saracens in the 2000-01 Tetley's Bitter Cup. Have Worcester got the all-round package to prosper in the top flight? The author believes so.

needs one or more investors who are prepared to finance such a budget of circa £1 million without any real expectation of seeing a financial return on that investment. Their motivation has to be simply a desire to be instrumental in enabling development and be associated with success. This need for independent financial support could be interpreted as an argument against automatic promotion. If such support is not available and all clubs in National Division One operate on a very low playing budget drawn from their own revenue resources, one club will still finish top of the pile at the end of the season and qualify for promotion, but they are unlikely then to be able to meet the criteria for survival in the Premiership, let alone for success.

In addition to substantial financial resources, a promoted club must have the potential to eventually attract regular crowds of between 6,000 and 12,000 people and have modern facilities that can cope comfortably with such numbers. The club must have the capacity and the vision to be able to generate significant additional revenue seven days a week throughout the year so that it becomes not only financially self-sufficient but also a sporting focal point for the community it serves. Ideally it should have an infrastructure that enables participation in the life of the club on many different levels, including age-group and amateur rugby. Sounds almost impossible doesn't it? But it isn't. I may be biased, but I believe Worcester are the only club in the National Divisions currently able to meet these requirements and bridge the gap. Only time will tell.

The author is chief executive of Worcester RFC

For over a decade Scottish Amicable have been proud to support the Barbarians and their unique style of rugby. The Scottish Amicable Tour 2001 saw one of the greatest Barbarian sides ever assembled thrill thousands of rugby fans throughout the UK with games against Wales, Scotland and England.

Scottish Amicable – supporting the game

POWER FOR THE FUTURE | Scottish Amicable

HOME SCENE

Wooden Spoon Society

GRANDSTAND FINISH:
the last Tetley's final

BY **ALASTAIR HIGNELL**

Falcons full back David Walder touches down in injury time to snatch victory for Newcastle in the Tetley's final.

In only one sense is it just as well that this was the last Tetley's Bitter Cup final. If there were to be any more, the sponsors would have to change the whole thrust of their advertising as well as the address of their website.

The latter suggests that the brewer does things smoothly. This match, featuring Newcastle and Harlequins, suggested the opposite. It was fast, ferocious, nerve-jangling and controversial. A 60,000 crowd could hardly have wished for better entertainment as an injury-time try by David Walder gave Newcastle their first cup success since 1977.

The size of the crowd was a tribute to the appeal of the competition and to the marketing efforts of the two finalists. It had been feared that switching the fixture from its traditional slot in mid-May to late February would deter some supporters. Its placement midway between Twickenham internationals against Italy and Scotland hardly helped, nor did the knowledge that neither club is among the better supported outfits in the Premiership. But both had proved throughout the season that they were cup specialists. Both were going well in the European Shield – indeed they were due to play each other in an April semi-final – and while erratic in the league, had saved their best performances for the Tetley's competition.

Newcastle had followed away victory at Rosslyn Park in the fourth round with three successive home wins over Premiership sides. Bristol went down 32-16 at Kingston Park, London Irish by 33 points to 20, while Sale were destroyed in the semi-final, the 37-25 scoreline even more comfortable than it looked. Quins had also started away, winning 36-8 at Plymouth Albion, and eased into the last eight with a 38-8 win at the Stoop against Manchester. Even though they were at home again for their quarter-final, few gave them much of a hope against the reigning European champions, Northampton. An 11-6 victory over the Saints was followed by an even more extraordinary, season-turning semi-final victory over Leicester.

Season-turning semi. Will Greenwood, who scored a try in the game, tries to offload to Steve White-Cooper as Harlequins put Leicester out of the cup at the semi-final stage.

The confidence engendered by a 22-18 win over the best team in the country ensured that whatever the clubs' respective Premiership positions – Quins were eleventh, Newcastle fifth – the London side were full of self-belief as they made the short trip across the A316. In captain David Wilson, they had Australia's most-capped flanker, with the priceless ability to be as destructive when the opposition had the ball as he was creative when his own team were in possession. Jason Leonard, the world's most-capped prop, was the cornerstone of a pack which also included Ireland's charismatic and in-form captain Keith Wood and the giant Australian Garrick Morgan; behind, England centre Will Greenwood was in the form of his life and Irish outside half Paul Burke was back after injury to pull the strings.

Newcastle, by contrast, could boast no more than a workmanlike pack, with captain Doddie Weir, fellow Scot Stuart Grimes and South African Marius Hurter providing the ballast, but behind them was a back line to die for. Veterans Gary Armstrong and Inga Tuigamala provided the experience, but from Jonny Wilkinson outwards, there was nothing but youthful exuberance. Centres Jamie Noon and Tom May had already been introduced to the England set-up, wing Michael Stephenson and full back David Walder were about to be. All four were in top form. All four were to be nominated as Premiership Young Players of the Season.

At first the final lived up to the simplistic prediction of a showdown between the Quins forwards and the Falcons backs. The Harlequins heavyweights dominated the opening exchanges without ever looking likely to score a try. By contrast Newcastle looked dangerous every time they could get their hands on the ball and scored from their first real attack, when a break from Tuigamala was carried on by Walder and finished off powerfully by May.

For all that, Quins were ahead 14-10 at half-time as, with Wilkinson and Burke swapping kicks, they fashioned a brilliant team try of their own, Wilson the ultimate beneficiary after a drive from the forwards and a cleverly timed pass from Greenwood. Quins were even further ahead after an hour. Burke had hit the post with his conversion attempt but when it came to taking penalties, he couldn't miss. Five successes from five, contrasting glaringly with two misses from four from Wilkinson, gave Quins a 20-13

David Wilson, the vastly experienced Australian captain of Harlequins, bears down on Jamie Noon, one of the young guns in the Falcons back line.

cushion as the game entered its closing stages. And Wilkinson's day got worse while Burke's got better, as the former failed with the conversion of May's second try and the latter skated over for his first ever try for Quins, converting it himself to put the Londoners nine points ahead.

Wilkinson missed another conversion as Newcastle came surging back – a break from Tuigamala allowing impressive No. 8 Jim Jenner to squeeze in at the corner. But Wilkinson's loss of form may ultimately have done the Falcons the favour they needed.

With the gap still at four points as the game entered injury time, Newcastle knew that only a try would do. A series of charges led to prop Ian Peel being bundled into touch five metres from the Quins line. Inexplicably, touch judge Steve Lander awarded the throw to Newcastle. From the line out, Wilkinson and Noon carved out enough space for Walder to blast through for the match-winning try. To rub salt into Quins wounds, Wilkinson suddenly rediscovered his kicking boots and converted it.

It was a sensational finish to arguably the best cup final of all time. Neither side deserved to lose, but perhaps Newcastle deserved to win because of the way they put their trust in the exciting, adventurous, risk-taking buccaneers behind the scrum.

Harlequins' Irish stand-off Paul Burke marks his return from injury by grabbing a cup final try, his first ever try for the club.

Right: Man of the match Va'aiga Tuigamala seems satisfied with his day's work as he celebrates Newcastle's dramatic victory with Liam Botham and try scorer David Walder.

Even so, it was particularly hard on Quins captain David Wilson, who took the field not quite fully fit, yet had contributed just about everything he could to ensure victory, including the first try, before he was forced off after an hour. It was hard too on Paul Burke, whose try was a gem and whose 22-point haul was a cup final record.

But it was a great way to go out for referee Ed Morrison. Deservedly put in charge of the Rugby World Cup final in 1995, the Bristolian has been the outstanding referee in the game ever since. This was his last major match at Twickenham. That it was such a brilliant and entertaining spectacle had a lot to do with the feel he has always had for the game and its players. He will be missed. The sponsors also deserve a fond farewell. Tetley's have decided to change direction and make this their final final. They could hardly have picked a more spectacular way to go.

But what of the competition itself? There was talk that switching the final to February was the first step towards phasing the National Knockout Cup out altogether. As it is, the new fixture list has placed the final at the end of April. If the tournament has been saved, as a genuine focus for the hopes and ambitions of every club in the land, it will owe a debt of gratitude not just to Tetley's, and Ed Morrison, but also to the players of Harlequins and Newcastle. They served up a reminder of how special, how good for the sport as a whole, a showpiece occasion can be.

A delighted Doddie Weir, the Newcastle captain, holds aloft the Tetley's Bitter Cup for the Falcons fans' approval.

TIGERS SEIZE TREBLE CHANCE: the 2001 Heineken Cup final

BY ALASTAIR HIGNELL

'Awesome.' Austin Healey got one thing absolutely spot on in an emotional and breathless post-match interview. Leicester's second-half fightback against the French champions was better than anything even they had managed in their three-year domination of the English game. Healey was named man of the match in Paris, but what carried Leicester home from 15-9 down at the break to score three scintillating tries and twice regain the lead was an unquenchable spirit that imbued every single player in the famous red, green and white shirt. The Leicester lip couldn't pass up the opportunity to criticise the ERC for choosing Parc des Princes – just a stone's throw from the Stade Français headquarters – as a neutral venue for this showpiece occasion, but he couldn't deny that the perceived injustice on the day fuelled Leicester to even greater heights and will in time move a stupendous achievement into the realms of legend.

Leicester's chief playmaker, Pat Howard, in his last match for the club, makes a break at the Parc de Princes.

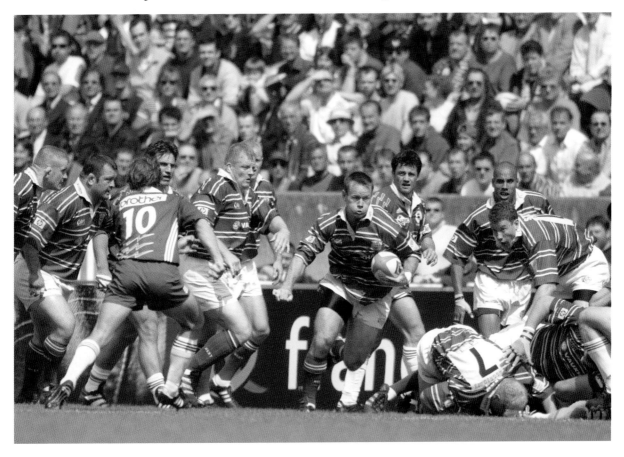

The Tigers were up against a formidable, all-international Stade pack, including back-rower Christophe Moni, here putting in a crunching tackle on Leicester skipper Martin Johnson.

Venue aside, this was a final that had been on the cards since the competition began back in October. Stade Français' millionaire backer Max Guazzini had made it clear that only Heineken Cup success was good enough for his expensively assembled squad. Leicester tried hard not to show it, but it rankled that both Bath and Northampton had beaten them to European glory and that their one appearance in the final had resulted in a good old-fashioned thumping from the Frenchmen of Brive.

Seeded behind holders Northampton, the English and French champions had made remarkably similar progress through the group stages. Both had lost in Wales – Leicester at Pontypridd, Stade at Swansea – and neither had been particularly extended in front of their own fans in the quarter-finals. Leicester crushed Swansea 41-10 to set up an all-English semi-final against Gloucester, while Stade brushed Pau aside 36-19 to clinch a meeting with Munster. Both teams received the shocks they needed in the semi-finals. Stade profited from a dodgy call from touch judge Steve Lander to survive a second-half onslaught from the Irishmen in Lille and win by a single point in 31, while Leicester also found themselves counting the clock down at Watford, before edging home 19-15.

Destiny, it seemed to the fans of both teams, was there to be grasped at the Parc des Princes on the third weekend in May. Leicester were on a roll, hard-fought Zurich Championship final success against Bath having taken them two-thirds of the way towards an unprecedented treble. Stade, by contrast, had gone down at Béziers to lose ground on Castres in the French Championship, but their fans had the shortest of trips to make and they could bank on a majority in the 45,000 capacity crowd.

The metronomic Diego Dominguez converted nine penalties and slotted a dropped goal to score all his side's points, but in the end it was not quite enough to deny Leicester a thrilling 34-30 win.

Both teams were just a wing short of full strength, Leicester ruling out Samoan international Freddie Tuilagi, and Stade unable to consider flying youngster Raphael Poulain. Even so, the Parisian side's starting line-up could boast 14 internationals from four countries, Leicester 11 from three.

For once, the Tigers were outpowered. Stade coach John Connolly had assembled an all-international juggernaut of a pack, with a front row, Sylvain Marconnet, Fabrice Landreau and Pieter de Villiers, who had played as a unit for France, and a back row featuring the bald-headed Christophe Moni, the captain Christophe Juillet and the in-form Englishman Richard Pool-Jones. Behind, he had chosen his best attacker, France

SAFE HANDS

www.cheltglos.co.uk

C&G Cheltenham & Gloucester

Looking after your best interests

C&G MORTGAGES

For a range of attractive mortgages and investment accounts, backed by a track record for value and outstanding service, just get in touch with Cheltenham & Gloucester.

For more details contact us on:

0800 272 131

Austin Healey steps inside Stade's Morgan Williams on his way to the man of the match award. Having been replaced at scrum half, Healey returned at fly half to create Leon Lloyd's match-winning second try.

wing Christophe Dominici, at full back and preferred the feisty Canadian Morgan Williams at scrum half.

It was clear from the outset how Connolly expected his team to play. Williams and outside half Diego Dominguez were to keep Stade going forward, the heavyweight eight were to apply the screw, and Dominguez would convert the pressure into points. And the tactics worked. The Italian international landed five penalties out of five, two from just inside his own half, while Leicester, seemingly discomforted by the occasion as well as by the opposition, found themselves kicking away what good ball they got and trailing 15-9 at the break.

Whatever was said at half-time certainly did the trick. Within a minute, Leicester had scored a stunning try. Austin Healey was thumped backwards in a tackle by Pool-Jones in midfield, but quick ball gave Pat Howard, in his last match for the Tigers, the opportunity to place an inch-perfect cross-kick into the arms of right wing Geordan Murphy. The Irishman found himself in space but knew he couldn't make the line so he slowed down to suck in the cover and poked a clever little grubber kick through for his team-mates to chase. Centre Leon Lloyd just beat Williams to the loose ball, recovered the quicker and touched down in the right corner.

It was a stunning score, but it didn't look to be decisive, especially when Tim Stimpson's failure to convert was followed by a frenetic quarter-hour in which Martin Johnson was yellow-carded, Austin Healey was injured and Dominguez landed two more penalties as well as missing one and fluffing a dropped-goal attempt.

Christophe Dominici, playing at full back, cannot stop Leon Lloyd touching down for his second try. Tim Stimpson's conversion meant Stade had to score a try to win. The Tigers held out.

But the game really was turned on its head midway through the second period. When Marconnet lost the ball in a charge into the Leicester half, Howard whipped it away to Lloyd, whose searing 50-metre break took him into the Stade 22. He was late-tackled by Dominici as he kicked ahead, but Healey took the tap penalty, Back burrowed over for the try, and Stimpson converted.

Leicester were level, and when Stimpson landed his fifth successful kick from six attempts, after a charge by Dorian West had been illegally halted, they went ahead for the first time in the match. They held that lead for less than a minute as the second highest points scorer in rugby history punished them straight from the restart with his eighth penalty. A ninth remorseless strike from Dominguez with nine minutes to go regained the lead for Stade and a nerveless dropped goal snatched it back for the third time after Stimpson's sixth successful kick. No one, it seemed, was going to spoil Dominguez' party.

Except for Healey. Obviously suffering from a knee injury, he had been replaced at scrum half by Jamie Hamilton, only to re-enter the fray at outside half in place of Andy Goode. With three minutes left on the clock, the England international looped Pat Howard at inside centre and somehow found the pace to go past Dominguez. A perfectly timed pass found Lloyd scorching up outside him for a magnificent second try.

Every bit as important as the try, however, was the conversion by Stimpson from wide out on the right. The four-point cushion it created ensured that when Stade threw the kitchen sink at the Tigers in the final few seconds, another Dominguez penalty would not be enough to give them victory. Stade were forced to run with the ball, and Leicester's defence, unbreached and unbreachable since the quarter-finals, was more than equal to the task – and the ten laps of honour that followed the final whistle.

Theirs is an unprecedented achievement and the celebrations and congratulations were fully deserved. But even as the cheers were dying down around the Parc, the Tigers were typically setting out to raise their own benchmark. Chief playmaker Pat Howard may be on his way back to Australia, and Healey may be flirting with a move to pastures new, but All Black legend Josh Kronfeld has already committed himself to the Tigers, and another Australian, Rod Kafer, may also be on his way to Welford Road. There he'll find an academy that is already the envy of the rest of the Premiership and a whole clutch of players who've had a taste of the top flight and not been found wanting. Not just for next season, but for some time to come, Leicester will be the team to beat.

Leicester's eight tenors treat the Parc des Princes crowd to an impromptu concert as the treble celebrations get underway.

HARLEQUINS: EURO
Harlequins 4

*Above: Quins lock
Garrick Morgan has his
progress interrupted.
Below: Quins skipper
David Wilson latches
on to Narbonne centre
Cristian Stoica. Right:
The victorious Quins
get the party rolling.*

AN SHIELD WINNERS
Narbonne 33

Above: Pat Sanderson, a Quins try scorer, runs at the Narbonne defence. Below: Hooker Keith Wood was fit again after missing the semi-final against Newcastle.

WHERE'S THE RETURN FOR THE WELSH CLUBS?

BY **EDDIE BUTLER**

Swansea's Rhodri Jones is tackled by Stephen Jones of Llanelli during the 1998-99 SWALEC Welsh Challenge Cup final at Ninian Park. The All Whites, with their experience against English clubs, defeated the Scarlets 37-10.

The most gruesome moment in the troubled early years of professional rugby came with the breakaway season of 1998-99, when Cardiff and Swansea cast themselves in the mould of rebels and opted out of Wales. The details of their row with the Welsh Rugby Union – something to do with a refusal to sign a ten-year loyalty agreement with the governing body – seem obscure, and certainly petty, now. But it is worth briefly returning to the theme of strife at the end of the last millennium, just to remind ourselves how much has changed in the first years of the 21st century.

At the time of Cardiff and Swansea's abandonment of their own parish, the English clubs were involved in a dispute of their own with the Rugby Football Union – and with ERC, the body that ran European competition. Such were the strains that England's top clubs, plus the Welsh rebels, opted out of European competition that season.

In a way, tensions are still more evident between Twickenham and the elite clubs of England than they are between their Welsh counterparts. Cardiff and Swansea soon enough found a compromise and made their peace with the WRU.

The English clubs, too, rejoined European competition. Indeed, the very next season Northampton were crowned Heineken champions. But over a year after the Saints' memorable day out at Twickenham there was still an item on the agenda to undo the very agreements that held the new professional game together. It would take yet another special general meeting to see off for the last time the counter-revolutionaries who saw professionalism as a curse on their beloved amateurism.

There was never such an ideological divide in Wales. Money had never been viewed as a pollutant, merely as something in short supply. From the outset of the new age in 1995, when the game went open, the Welsh Rugby Union seemed willing to step in to provide financial assistance.

Llanelli and Neath were given such assistance that the WRU could claim to be the owners of the clubs. This in itself might have led to problems, since it seemed help was on offer to clubs that had spent their way into trouble. Clubs like Newport, who had kept their balance sheet in order but had seen their fortunes on the field consequently suffer, looked on with no mean degree of astonishment as aid was delivered to the very clubs who had spent money they did not have on recruiting the Black and Ambers' finest players. In general, however, such practices were tolerated as the inevitable consequences of being plunged headlong into a commercial world. The clubs' loyalty had been bought. Only Cardiff and Swansea settled for the rebel route.

They were accepted into a halfway house. The English clubs played them but could not include them in their official league table. To do so would have put them in breach of agreement, and they were not quite ready to break away from Twickenham. The English clubs could not even afford to put out their strongest sides in their Welsh 'friendlies'. The money on offer in the Allied Dunbar Premiership was more important than solidarity.

The English clubs paraded their second strings and were soundly beaten. On the rare occasions when they did play at full strength the games were raw and tense. 'Rebels with a cause' was the rallying cry, competition among equals the assessment of the balance of power between England and Wales.

Cardiff and Swansea in that strange season of dislocation still played in the Welsh Challenge Cup. Swansea met Llanelli in the final. The clubs that had remained loyal had been pretty rude about the rebels. This was a chance to see who, if anyone, had made more progress in limbo. Scott Gibbs of Swansea said that playing against the English clubs had helped enormously. It would be men against boys. It was. Swansea won easily.

The following season the rebels were back in the fold. What was needed now was to take the giant leap that had been begging to be made for years: create an Anglo-Welsh league. Now, however, the word was coming down from Clive Woodward and England at international level that there could be no benefit at all in generating a new structure that would serve only the interests of Wales. There was nothing in it for England.

Such an attitude did nothing to improve relations between the club owners, who by now resented any form of interference in their affairs, and Twickenham. But it was an astute observation. Wales needed England more than England needed Wales.

The Anglo-Welsh became the Welsh/Scottish. England continued on their upward path. Wales – and Scotland – became bogged down in a premiership lacking the bite that goes with taking on the real enemy, England.

All was not lost. There was still European competition. In the season after Northampton's victory, Cardiff found themselves pooled alongside Saracens, Swansea alongside Wasps. Cardiff beat Saracens home and away, and Swansea overwhelmed

Wasps on the sandy soil of St Helen's. It seemed that the Welsh had lost none of their ability to turn it on against the English.

But England were only briefly wilting. The international players who had been on the go non-stop for two years were taking a breather in the early days of the 2000-01 season. Soon they were playing flat out, setting a standard that was embraced by many others in the Zurich Premiership.

By the time of the quarter-finals early in 2001 it was clear the balance had swung the other way. Gloucester, struggling for form in the weekly grind of the English Premiership, beat first Llanelli and then Cardiff. The latter game, in particular, was ugly for Welsh eyes. Gloucester reduced the game to a squeeze on the Cardiff pack, and a team bristling with Test players had no response. Swansea were swept aside by Leicester in an even more emphatic declaration that the Welsh could not live with the English clubs. It created a climate that spilt into the Six Nations Championship. England were on fire; Wales allowed them to dictate from first to last.

South African centre Pieter Muller tries in vain to latch on to Andrew Dall during Cardiff's clash with the Edinburgh Reivers in the 2000-01 Welsh/Scottish League. Opposite page: the ups and downs of the Welsh clubs' European campaign – Emyr Lewis bursts through two Saracens defenders as Cardiff win 32-23 at Vicarage Road (above); Sililo Martens gets the ball away as Swansea go down 41-10 to the Tigers (below).

The mood has changed in just three years. Wales were once England's equals. Now they have been left behind. And the gulf is alarmingly wide. England's clubs may have their ongoing spats with authority, but they are bristling with purpose on the field and are threatening to break even any day now.

In Wales the shadow of the events of January and February have left scars. The crowds are nothing like those who flock to Welford Road to watch Leicester. The feeling is that the English have slipped out of reach.

Or have they? Bridgend and Newport have generous owners in the shape of Leighton Samuel and Tony Brown, and even if their input is not on the scale of Nigel Wray's at Saracens then the cost of living in South Wales does not compare with running a club in London. Wales has its sugar daddies.

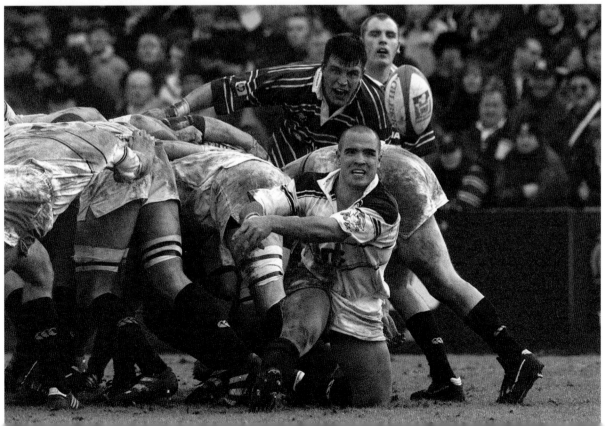

But the nature of development and improvement of rugby clubs has changed. One man's money is no longer the blueprint for success. Leicester have changed all that. They have sponsors in the city that might be the envy of some of the towns of the old coal belt 200 miles west but basically are a rugby club reliant on no one figure. Leicester is a rugby town. It oozes rugby and the crowds share the passions of the players – their family – with all the fervour that used to go with being a supporter of Llanelli.

It is one of the ironies – and only too typical perhaps – that Wales used to have a club like Leicester. Pontypridd were the standard-bearers for a never-say-die commitment that proved more unifying than any fat-cat salaries. So strong was the Ponty home-grown feeling that they were the only club to beat Leicester in the pool stages of the European Cup in the year of the Tigers' triumph.

But Ponty did not qualify for next season's Heineken Cup. They slowly slipped down the Welsh/Scottish League until they were out of the top five. That is the irony. The Ponty spirit is the Leicester spirit and it is the way ahead.

A sugar daddy is very handy, but the sense of community comes first. Tony Brown of Newport understands this. He rolls up his sleeves and sells the programmes on match day. He sells his club as much as he owns it.

Ben Cohen puts distance between himself and Mark Taylor during England's 44-15 2001 Six Nations victory at the Millennium Stadium. Symbolic of a widening gulf between Welsh and English rugby in general?

Such a commitment only promises a bright future. Wales has struggled in the early years of professionalism, but it is not as if rugby was ever truly threatened with extinction. It had a bad patch and it will have bad patches again in the future. But the crowds will come back, because rugby is in the blood. And just as it is in the adult community of Pontypridd so it is in the genes of the youngsters. Wales continues to pour out talent. It remains one of the great nurseries of the world. Now that rugby offers a career path, Wales will only become a more vibrant hotbed.

When professionalism first shook rugby from top to toe, money was everything. Money was the lifeblood and money was the poison. From the hyperinflation of salaries to rebel wages, money, money, money. Well, it's still there making the professional game go round in its strange oval way, but it is no longer the grass on which a cow must feed. It is merely the fertiliser that will determine whether that grass is lush or a bit dry.

In Wales there may not be much money. The dream of purchased glory will never come true. But success can be built organically. Not much money in Wales, but plenty of rain. The grass will grow and rugby will be played on it.

Crowds flock to Welford Road, Leicester – headquarters of a rugby town. Such fervour and dedication still exists in Wales and is the way forward for Welsh rugby.

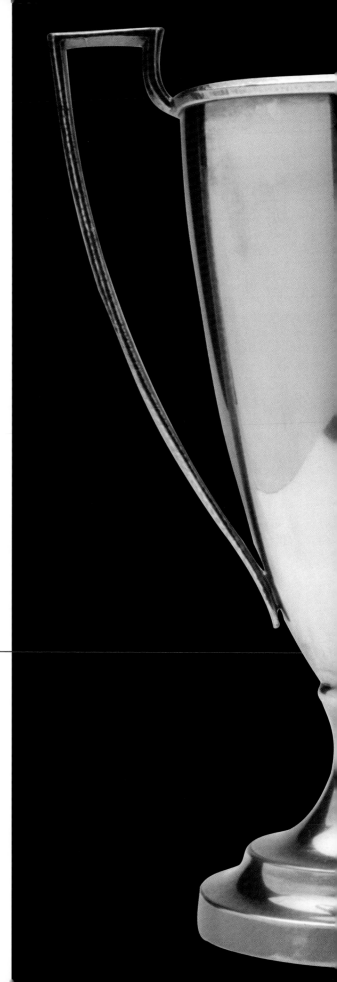

A top team in the field of law.
One step ahead of the game.

winning

Wragge&Co

55 Colmore Row Birmingham B3 2AS England
Telephone +44(0)121 233 1000 Fax +44(0)121 214 1099
e-mail: mail@wragge.com   website: www.wragge.com

WOODWARD'S ENGLAND VISION

BY **MARK SOUSTER**

As first and foremost a fan to the core, Clive Woodward recalls vividly the feeling of being cheated, of England's long-suffering rugby public being short-changed after another predictable but ultimately unsatisfactory victory at Twickenham. 'Time and time again I remember going to the West Car Park even after a win with a hollow feeling. We were winning, but something was missing,' said Woodward. 'Some of the games didn't turn me on. It was boring rugby. I thought to myself then about what I would do if I was in charge but obviously never dreamt I would be.'

Fast-forward a decade, and out of the blue, lady luck came calling. England gambled on the rookie coach – who admits he had to find his feet in the unforgiving public glare and who had only just started at Bath – and came up trumps. 'It was a risky appointment, I was inexperienced, but whoever chose me realised I was a guy who could adapt. We are a long way from the finished article. There was no template because having a template means you are copying from somebody else. I hadn't a clue when I started, to be frank, how it was going to work out. But I had confidence in my own ability to learn quickly. Nobody really knew me. I just hope I have shocked a few people in a pleasant way.'

England coach Clive Woodward: 'My objective is to make England the best rugby team in the world.'

With Woodward the driving force, England are playing the brand of rugby that has other nations, particularly those in the southern hemisphere, raising their heads and sniffing the breeze with a mixture of concern and respect. After years of bumbling along, of shooting themselves in the foot, England inexorably are moving in the right direction. Woody has created an elite structure, a vision of sporting excellence which once tasted, no one in their right mind would want to leave. A golden era beckons, and for that he must take most of the credit, although he is quick to emphasise it is about teamwork – the players, obviously, who have thrived in the competitive environment, the coaches, the support staff, the management at Twickenham who stood by him when others were calling for his head after the World Cup.

He has nothing but praise for the support he has received in the corridors at Twickenham, where the internecine politicking makes the Vatican seem like a parish council in comparison. 'I have tremendous backing from Francis Baron [chief executive]. He has said no to me loads of times and we have had our moments, but he is a great guy to work for.'

One of Woodward's new generation of crowd-pleasers, Iain Balshaw, leaves everyone in his wake as he heads for the line during England's 66-23 Six Nations win over Italy at Twickenham in 2001.

Woodward continued: 'When I got the opportunity I was determined I was not not going to take risks in trying to achieve what I wanted to achieve. You have got to stick your head out. I've been whacked a few times, but I am still here. But I have learned. Now I feel totally in control of anything that can be thrown at me on and off the field in terms of how I run it. It takes time and experience. The coaches around me are learning as well, so hopefully when one of them gets a chance to be the main guy they won't have to go through what I went through starting from scratch.'

Now he finds watching England a thrill. 'Seeing players doing things off the cuff, to have genuine crowd-pleasers to excite is what it is all about. People like Iain Balshaw, Jonny Wilkinson, Austin Healey, Mike Catt – it's brilliant.'

Woodward is positively bubbling with excitement at what lies ahead. Crucial to England's continued development is the challenge posed by the giants of SANZAR, with whom there is occasionally talk of a four nations championship. 'As a coach I much prefer England to be playing Australia, South Africa or New Zealand far more than the Six Nations. The Six Nations is important for British rugby, but I prefer the challenge of going into games where you are not favourites. But I am a big fan of the Six Nations. I grew up with it. It is a difficult tournament for England, as it is five cup finals. I would hate to see it go. As long as we have the fixtures with SANZAR each year as well, the programme is perfect.'

Woodward denies that being overlooked by the Lions this summer lent extra urgency to his desire to make a point. 'I looked at the Lions in the cold light of day. It was the right decision. I am glad I have been here. This has been a very important summer for England. My place is as England coach and I have no qualms about that. The decision was correct and I am in my rightful place. I would have been distracted in Australia.'

On the broader front it is an exciting time to be part of the Woodward roller coaster. In his world, in which he has drawn heavily from his business background, there are certain rules and parameters, but thereafter there are no rules. While the RFU has a strategic plan, his is to win the next game. People are encouraged to question, experiment. 'I don't think I am English in many ways. I have no problem questioning the status quo. There are no rules in business [he used to run a leasing company] and I have adopted that philosophy in rugby. There are no rules in rugby. There is no reason why I can't do anything, such as take on specialist coaches. Once you get that through, you start to be successful. That is what I have tried to instil in the players and staff. Just because we have always done it that way doesn't mean it is right.

'My objective is to make England the best rugby team in the world. You have got to have that attitude. We are genuinely getting there, purely based on our financial strength, our club strength and the number of players. And if we really do concentrate on elite performance and elite development, there is no reason why we can't be the best team in the world. I can't see the success stopping. Everything is in place.'

Although referee Andre Watson called for video evidence, touch judge Clayton Thomas is in no doubt that Dan Luger has touched down to bring Woodward's England a last-gasp victory over the world champion Wallabies at Twickenham in November 2000.

BARBARIAN INVASION: the Scottish Amicable Tour 2001

BY CHRIS JONES

Like an aged favourite aunt who appears to be out of time with her surroundings, the Barbarians seemed destined to fade away from the rugby spotlight when professionalism arrived. The only question was where would the most famous invitation side in the world find a suitable retirement home for all those stars? In fact, the arrival of the professional game has seen the stock of the Barbarians rise, and they have now found a new place in the hearts of fans, particularly those who were hoping to see England taken down a peg or two this year.

The Barbarians are now a key part of the end of each northern hemisphere season, with thousands of fans packing the Millennium Stadium, Murrayfield and Twickenham this year to watch a host of world-class players run in hatfuls of tries. The Scottish Amicable tour also allowed men like Gary Teichmann and Gary Pagel to wave goodbye to British rugby on an appropriate stage as they headed home for retirement in South Africa.

Jonah Lomu, supported by Josh Kronfeld and Gary Teichmann, runs into Kyran Bracken during the Barbarians' 43-29 win over England at Twickenham.

Given England's unbeaten form in 2001, the Twickenham fixture was always going to be the centre of attention once national team manager Clive Woodward had enthusiastically agreed to take over the match from Leicester, the champions. It formed the first game on England's short summer tour and allowed a squad missing 18 players on Lions duty to gel before taking on Canada and the USA.

For Wales, the BaaBaas first opponents, and for Scotland it was a case of getting the best possible sides out on the pitch and hoping the invitation squad would not be able to function for three successive matches in a week – some hope! Wales coach Graham Henry ensured the opening game would be a real contest by picking many of the Lions players he would be taking to Australia. The Millennium Stadium was in the middle of an amazingly busy football period, with cup finals and play-off matches to be fitted in, and the new pitch stood up well to the pounding.

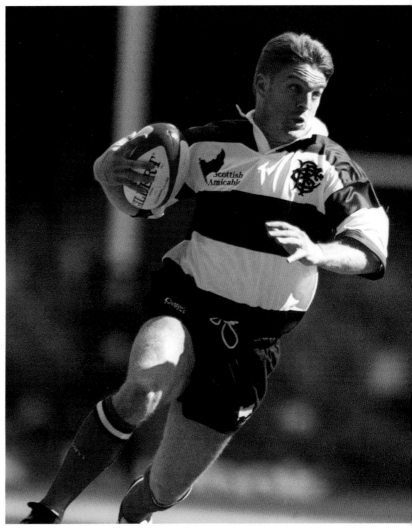

Critically for the Lions, the match allowed England wing Dan Luger a much-needed outing for the Barbarians after his neck injury, which he suffered on the same pitch when he ran into Scott Gibbs during the Six Nations match between Wales and England. Luger signalled his return to the big time with an early try in a match that saw Tim Horan, who won the World Cup with Australia at Cardiff in 1999, replacing his Wallaby team-mate Jason Little, also a 1999 World Cup winner, in the second half. These two great Australian backs will be badly missed at Test level by everyone who enjoys watching a truly world-class midfield combination operating together.

Wales appeared to have pulled off a dramatic win when Stephen Jones kicked an 81st-minute penalty to give his side a 38-33 lead. The crowd were not happy with the decision to kick, believing it was against the BaaBaas spirit, and they turned their full support behind Teichmann's Barbarians team. The result was a sensational late try, the second for Blue Bulls flyer Friedrich Lombard, which meant Braam van Straaten had to kick the touch-line conversion for victory.

Double World Cup winner, former Wallaby centre Tim Horan in action against Wales in Cardiff.

With the kind of accuracy that has allowed him to set all kinds of records back home in South Africa, the outside half put the ball between the posts to secure a great win by 40 points to 38. 'Who dares wins' had been the BaaBaas' motto and it had brought another victory.

If a near full-strength Welsh team could not stop the BaaBaas, what price the underachieving Scots at Murrayfield? A poor season had brought call-ups to the Lions for only three of the Scotland squad and despite having the rest of his players to choose from, Ian McGeechan was given an uncomfortable 80 minutes in this evening match. The BaaBaas stormed to a 74-31 win, with Jonah Lomu giving notice of his return to fitness by scoring four tries and making three more for team-mates. What a return!

Lomu was just too powerful on the hoof for the Scottish defence, and the only crumbs of comfort for the home side were the performances in defeat of Marcus Di Rollo at centre and flanker Donnie Macfadyen. Thanks to these two, Scotland found themselves, rather surprisingly, leading 19-15. This only served to fire up Lomu for even greater feats and the visitors led 41-26 at the break. The BaaBaas ran in 12 tries to thrill the youngsters in the crowd and substantially boost Scottish Amicable's contribution to charity.

It is a measure of how the BaaBaas have maintained their standing in the world game that against Scotland they fielded a half-back combination of Percy Montgomery and Joost van der Westhuizen, as well as Lomu on the wing, Horan at centre, and Robin Brooke, Pat Lam and Ben Clarke in a hard-working pack. No wonder the Scots wilted!

Twickenham produced a 50,000 crowd for a non-cap England match to signal the completion of the domestic season and the end of the BaaBaas' short tour. Fireworks welcomed the players onto the pitch and they continued in the game, with referee Clayton Thomas having to remind players that this was a BaaBaas match, so would they stop killing the ball and thumping each other!

Craig Dowd looks on as his Barbarians team-mate Pat Lam picks up and goes in the invitation side's 40-38 victory at the Millennium Stadium.

It was, as BaaBaas coach Bob Dwyer admitted afterwards, the most ferocious fixture the invitation side had been involved in for many years. England, minus their Lions players, sent out a side containing experienced old hands like Kyran Bracken and Julian White and new boys such as Dave Walder and Michael Stephenson, both of Newcastle.

It was appropriate that the first try of the match should be claimed by BaaBaas centre Pat Howard, the outstanding player in England last season. Howard has now returned to Australia in search of Test caps after helping Leicester to an incredible treble. He easily sidestepped England captain Bracken for a touchdown that van Straaten converted, but there were very few easy scores after that.

Both sides refused to take a backward step, which saw Josh Kronfeld, playing his last representative match before joining Leicester, constantly in the wrong place at the right time. England punched and kicked him back onto his own side of the rucks and mauls and the referee also tried to nullify this amazing flanker. Kronfeld was only doing what comes naturally to him, and England were just as guilty of trying to slow down possession. It was played like any other Test match at Twickenham.

The BaaBaas strolled to a 19-3 lead thanks to a Joeli Vidiri try and a clever piece of play between Howard and Jeremy Guscott, the England hero. Guscott was making his final appearance at Twickenham and after coming on as a replacement for Little caught a neat chip ahead by Howard to glide in under the posts for a try that was greeted with thunderous applause. To England's credit, they refused to let the BaaBaas get too far ahead and after conceding a Lomu try in the 28th minute fashioned a great score for Wasps full back Paul Sampson. He injured his back going over at the corner but carried

A touch of the old Guscott magic carries the former England favourite past Dorian West, Alex King and Joe Worsley. Guscott scored a highly popular try in this his last game at Twickenham.

Brimming over with class and firepower. The Barbarians squad pose for the camera after their encounter with a depleted but game England that BaaBaas coach Bob Dwyer described as 'the most physical encounter I have seen with the BaaBaas'.

on for the rest of the match, England running out of replacements as the pace and power of the game told on everyone.

A Pat Lam try early in the second half took the score to 29-15 in favour of the Barbarians, but England worked Stephenson over for a neat try that Walder converted and the home side sensed a possible victory over star-studded opposition. There were only seven points in it when the BaaBaas put captain Teichmann over in the corner and van Straaten converted from wide out with outstanding accuracy.

Replacement centre Ben Johnston scored for England before suffering a knee injury that would rule him out of the North America tour. Nevertheless, it was appropriate that the visitors brought down the curtain on an absorbing contest with an Adrian Garvey try, created by another Lomu charge. The 43-29 winning margin was harsh on England but a clear indication of the scoring power the BaaBaas had at their disposal.

For Dwyer it was an outstanding return on a week's hard work during which many of the game's great names had produced world-class form in the famous black-and-white hooped jerseys. The BaaBaas had triumphed in all three games and provided a fitting end to a memorable season.

It was left to the softly spoken Teichmann to sum up the Lomu contribution: 'Jonah is pretty awesome and the only way you can try and control him is to deny him space. He is very fit and strong at the moment and is looking for the ball all the time. It is fantastic playing with him and a real problem playing against him!'

Dwyer added: 'The England game was the most physical encounter I have seen with the BaaBaas, and the scrums and rucks were particularly keenly fought. If anyone thought these games weren't for real then they now know the truth. This was a fair dinkum game.'

PENSIONS INVESTMENTS PROTECTION MORTGAGE SOLUTIONS
CONTACT YOUR FINANCIAL ADVISER FOR ALL THE ANSWERS

SECURE

Scottish Amicable is regulated by the Personal Investment Authority

POWER FOR THE FUTURE | Scottish Amicable

RUGBY WORLDWIDE

THE LIONS V THE WALLABIES

BY CHRIS JONES

Series turning point? Wallaby left wing Joe Roff intercepts Jonny Wilkinson's pass and scores in the corner despite the efforts of Brian O'Driscoll.

When history took a long, hard look at the 1989 Lions tour to Australia, one incident stood out as the series decider, and clips of what became known as David Campese's worst moment in Test rugby were replayed at each of the Tests during the 2001 tour. Australians appeared to enjoy putting themselves and Campese through the mill by constantly showing his awful pass to Greg Martin in the third Test, which fell to the ground and allowed Ieuan Evans, the Wales wing, to score the decisive try.

Time does heal all wounds, and by the time the 2001 Lions under Martin Johnson's outstanding leadership arrived in Australia, a cottage industry had grown up around the Campese try. Campo, who for so long bemoaned the constant mentioning of his mistake, appeared in a sponsor's advert which used his terrible error as part of the hard sell. The man himself even hosted a dinner for 600 guests where they paid to listen to him go through it all again.

When history gives its verdict on the 2001 Lions tour, there will be three potential errors that could fulfil the same role that Campese's blunder took. The trio of mistakes helped turn an engrossing series on its head and left the Wallabies with victory and the Lions with a battle-weary squad of losers.

The series-turning mistakes did not hit the Lions until after they had opened the rubber with a marvellous victory in Brisbane on the Gabba cricket ground. The Lions had suggested they could score from long range, but no one expected them to succeed with this tactic against the best defensive side in the world. Irish centres Rob Henderson and the mercurial Brian O'Driscoll made a mockery of the Wallaby defence, bursting through at will. Their efforts followed a try after three minutes of the first Test by England wing Jason Robinson – his first touchdown in a Test match since switching over from rugby league. Robinson then popped up on the other wing to make the most of an O'Driscoll surge to put Dafydd James clear, and suddenly the Lions led 12-3 at half-time with their hordes of red-shirted followers in fantastic voice. The stadium was decked out with hundreds of Welsh, English, Irish and Scottish flags, along with banners announcing to those watching at home that their friends and local rugby clubs were on the tour.

The Lions then unleashed O'Driscoll on a long-range run that ended in a brilliant solo try in the second minute of the second half, and the game was effectively over. Matt Dawson, the England scrum half, had chosen to air complaints about the tour management just before kick-off in an English national newspaper, and those words were made to look ridiculous as the Lions dominated the match.

The Lions led 29-3 in the 51st minute, and despite Wallaby tries from Andrew Walker and Nathan Grey plus a Walker penalty, this was the Lions' day. Scott Quinnell had barged over for the fourth Lions try, and Jonny Wilkinson kicked three conversions and a penalty to send the travelling hordes delirious with a 29-13 win.

It was all going so well that not even Dawson's badly timed comments appeared to hurt the party, which had already recovered from an earlier midweek loss to Australia A and the departure due to injury of Mike Catt, Lawrence Dallaglio and Dan Luger. The

Brian O'Driscoll slices through the Wallaby defence on his way to a long-range solo try early in the second half of the first Test.

Flanker Neil Back is helped to his feet after crossing for the Lions in the the second Test following a line-out drive.

final figure of seriously injured sent home would reach eight, but those very dark days were still to come. For now, it was on to Canberra and a last-gasp win with a conversion from Dawson as he went from villain to hero in a matter of days. That win, in the final midweek match, appeared to give the Lions an extra edge, while the Wallabies worried about outside half Stephen Larkham's arm injury.

The second Test in Melbourne featured two of the vital mistakes alluded to above, and they came just after half-time to dramatically change the balance of power in the series. At that stage, the Wallabies were reeling on the ropes, having gone in at half-time trailing 11-6 under the closed roof of the Colonial Stadium in Melbourne. The Lions should have been even further ahead but allowed try-scoring opportunities to slip away and had only two Wilkinson penalties and a Neil Back try from a line-out drive to show for their efforts, while the Wallabies had kicked two penalties through Burke. However, the Lions' overall play suggested it would be just a question of time before they repeated the incisive running that had brought success in the opening match of the three-Test series. Then disaster struck – twice.

First, Wilkinson, the England outside half, opted to pass to Rob Henderson with a three-to-one overlap on the short side, barely two minutes after the restart. Instead of reaching Henderson, Wilkinson only managed to float the ball into the hands of the leaping Joe Roff, one of the most dangerous wingers in world rugby. Roff gratefully accepted the gift and set off on a powerful 30-metre run that ended with him scoring despite a great attempted tackle by Ireland's O'Driscoll. The stadium erupted, but for the first time it was Wallaby supporters making noise rather than the 18,000 Lions fans who had made the long journey. Nevertheless, there didn't seem to be any reason for those Lions fans or the team to panic, even when Burke kicked a penalty to put the home side ahead, 14-11, for the first time in the series.

The second costly mistake was committed by the entire Lions pack as they failed to concentrate on a scrum outside their 22. The Wallabies suddenly twisted and drove until the Lions were sent spinning in all directions. The ball bounced into captain John Eales's hands and it reached Roff, who left opposite number Dafydd James for dead and then jinked inside two covering tacklers for Burke to convert.

The Wallabies, so woeful in the opening half, now led 21-11 after just ten minutes of the second half, and you could see the entire team gratefully accept this massive injection of much-needed confidence. The momentum had shifted away from the Lions and now sat easily with the Wallabies.

In a remarkable repeat of the first Test, the Wallabies put together a 29-3 scoring sequence to prove that anything the Lions could do, this band of all-gold brothers could

Martin Johnson, the first man to captain two consecutive Lions tours, as portrayed by leading caricaturist John Ireland.

The Expedia Lionesses
and Gareth, who
followed the Lions with
much media attention,
go through their routine
at half-time at Bruce
Stadium, Canberra.

match under Eales's leadership. Not even a penalty from Wilkinson could drag the Lions back from the brink of defeat, and Burke was on target with four kicks of his own to give the Wallabies a deserved 35-14 victory to square the series.

It wasn't just the Lions morale that was badly hurt by the defeat. Flanker Richard Hill was concussed by Nathan Grey's illegal use of the elbow, and the citing officer stunned everyone by letting the centre off without a ban. This was ludicrous given the two-match suspension Wales flanker Colin Charvis had to serve for using his knee on an opponent during the first Test. Rightly, Phil Larder, the Lions defensive coach, attacked the decision to let Grey off. It was a scandal, and not even claims that Larkham had been roughed up by the visitors in the second Test could deflect from this awful incident.

The Lions also lost their half-back pairing of Wilkinson and Rob Howley during the game. Howley suffered a cracked rib when a team-mate fell on him during the mayhem the Wallabies created in the final quarter of that second Test, while Wilkinson appeared to have suffered a broken left leg and was taken from the field on a stretcher. It was a truly awful night for the Lions, but it had squared the series, setting up a titanic decider at Stadium Australia in Sydney, where 84,000 fans would create a record attendance for a Lions match.

Given that the 2001 Lions tour was hampered by serious injury to key players throughout, it was not surprising to discover that a third of the Test side were carrying knocks and unable to train in the week before the decider. Will Greenwood, the England centre, was supposed to be on the replacements' bench, but his ankle injury flared up again, robbing him of a Lions Test debut in the series. Austin Healey became the dominant man in the week thanks to an X-ray which showed the Leicester utility back had a disc problem, making it impossible for him to replace James on the right wing. While all that was happening, Healey's column appeared in a British national newspaper, and he personally attacked Justin Harrison, the new Wallaby lock. It was an unnecessary act, which led to Healey being asked to appear before a Lions disciplinary panel after the tour to explain his actions. That article gave the Wallabies, and Harrison in particular, all the extra motivation they needed.

The other effect of Healey was that his injury left the squad with just one fit scrum half, Dawson. That meant the management had to call up Scotland veteran Andy Nicol to sit on the bench. He was in Sydney as a tour party leader and was seen avidly reading the line-out calls listed on pieces of paper in the hours before kick-off. Thankfully, he wasn't needed, although Dawson was kicked in the hamstring and forced to ice his left leg throughout the match.

During the week before the decider, the Wallabies lost Larkham to that arm injury and also lock Dave Giffin, the event which allowed Harrison to make a remarkable debut. Elton Flatley took over from Larkham and did an excellent job on a night of high emotions that also featured a thunderous fireworks show before kick-off.

Johnson, the Lions captain, knew his men had to pull away early and hold onto their lead against a Wallabies team that was still there for the taking. The Lions scrum was back to its fearsome best, but the line out did not function so well and raised the worry that the Wallabies had cracked the Lions call-sign code.

Both teams scored a try in the first half, Robinson getting his tenth tour touchdown for the Lions while Daniel Herbert finished off an excellent move for the Wallabies. The respective boots of Wilkinson, who had made a remarkable recovery under the guidance of Lions doctor James Robson, and Burke added the rest of the points, with the home side going into the break with a 16-13 advantage.

Jason Robinson beats the covering George Gregan to touch down for the first Lions try in the third Test. It was the Sale wing's tenth try of the tour.

It was vital the Lions started strongly in the final half of the match (and the tour). Wilkinson sped over for a neat try after two minutes, and his conversion suggested the series was within the visitors' grasp. However, the Lions again hit what had turned out to be a recurring problem – scoring points in the final 20 minutes of the Tests. Their last points in this deciding Test came in the 53rd minute through a Wilkinson penalty,

Very front row.

Strong Performance. **Solid** Delivery. **Disciplined** Investment Process.

Individual Savings Accounts (ISAs), PEP transfers, Pensions and Savings Plans, Investment Trusts and Open Ended Funds, Private Client Portfolio Management, Institutional Fund Management.

One of the largest independent fund management groups in the UK with £8.1 billion of funds under management.

Edinburgh
FUND MANAGERS
ROCK **SOLID**
Regulated by IMRO and the Personal Investment Authority.

www.edfd.com   **0800 028 6789**

whereas the Wallabies, showing greater fitness and staying power, pulled ahead to claim the series with another Herbert try and two penalties and a conversion from Burke.

With the match entering injury time, there was still a chance for the Lions to save themselves, but it was at this point that the third and final mistake of the series occurred. The Lions kicked a penalty to within 15 metres of the Wallaby line, and their 20,000 fans in the spectacular stadium sensed this was set up for another line-out catch and drive by their heroes. The Wallabies had been penalised earlier for pulling the maul down, and referee Paddy O'Brien could have awarded a penalty try if the home side opted to stop the Lions in a similar fashion. If they won the line out…

The call was for a short throw by Keith Wood to Johnson at the front. This is normally the safest option in world rugby, but no one had told Harrison, the new cap in the Wallaby second row. Harrison refused to listen to the other Wallaby forwards, who

Daniel Herbert dives in for the first of his two tries in the third Test. The Wallaby centre had an incident-packed match, since he also spent a period in the sin bin for a high tackle on Brian O'Driscoll.

were demanding that no one jumped against the Lions to ensure penalties were not conceded. Harrison backed himself to do something special. Wood threw the ball in and it was too low. Johnson didn't get to it first because Harrison's huge left hand grabbed the ball, and the Wallaby lock held onto it despite crashing to the ground. The stands erupted with Wallaby cheers because this last-ditch turnover effectively settled the match and the series. The Lions had, literally, thrown away their chance to make rugby history.

To pinpoint three mistakes as the keys to a series of so many injuries, incidents and examples of individual brilliance is harsh. But Test rugby is a harsh environment and chances have to be taken, despite the massive risk. Sadly for Johnson and his injury-ravaged Lions the errors were too costly, and it was Eales who gratefully accepted the Tom Richards Cup and a first series success over the Lions.

Above: Matt Cockbain (left) and debutant and man of the match Justin Harrison hug the Tom Richards Cup after the third Test. Right: Thanks for the memories. Wallaby coach Rod Macqueen, with captain John Eales, salutes the crowd at the end of his final match in charge.

IN PURSUIT OF RUGBY PERFECTION: Jonny Wilkinson

BY **SARAH MOCKFORD**

The party at the outset of the 2001 Lions tour of Australia comprised the top 37 rugby players from the four home nations. Yet among so many great players there was one young man who stood out and could be justifiably described as a rugby phenomenon. Jonny Wilkinson is one of the most dedicated, ambitious and focused rugby professionals of this era, and at only 22 he's already England's top scorer, with 407 points in only 27 internationals. On his first Lions tour Wilkinson faced a huge challenge against the world champion Wallabies. The expectation of the British and Irish fans was that he could win the Test series for them, as his talent and skill make him one of the most complete players in the sport.

Wilkinson strokes the ball goalwards in the first Australia v Lions Test at the Gabba, 2001.

The young fly half showed huge commitment to being part of the Test team in order to fight back from an injury suffered in Melbourne to be part of the final game in Sydney. He was a key figure in the final Test, scoring 18 points for the Lions. Unfortunately the victory was not to be, and the image of a tearful Wilkinson on his knees after the final whistle at Stadium Australia is one that will be remembered in years to come.

'The Lions against Australia is huge – it's as big as it gets. They are the world champions and the Tri-Nations champions, so they are the best in the world at the moment, and it makes it really special to be part of the Test team. It's something I certainly won't ever forget.'

Wilkinson had wanted to play for England ever since he can remember and he reached this goal in 1998 at the age of 18,

Wilkinson looks to offload as he is tackled by Martin Leslie during the 2001 Calcutta Cup match at Twickenham. Already, at 22, the fly half is England's top points scorer.

becoming the youngest capped player for 71 years. Once he established himself in the England side he knew there was only one other honour that was higher than playing for his country and that was to go on tour with the British & Irish Lions, which he accomplished this summer. 'It's like achieving a lifelong goal really. It's certainly not to be taken for granted, and it's an opportunity not to be wasted.'

The English fly half is renowned for being totally committed to improving his game, so the Lions tour was something that he tried to learn as much as possible from. 'You don't want to let an opportunity go. You know you've worked hard to get here, and there's absolutely no point in standing off now and letting everything fall away. I've worked hard, I've been through a lot of pain, and now I want to take it a step further.'

Wilkinson lives and breathes rugby, and he is dedicated to the pursuit of perfection, although he acknowledges that no matter how single-minded a player may be, he can always be better. Wilkinson recognises that he has little time away from rugby, but he does not seem to mind and finds simple ways to relax. 'When I've needed time to sit down and relax – which I often do, as I do get carried away – then I've been able to do that and

Training with the British & Irish Lions at Aldershot ahead of the trip Down Under. Of his selection for the Lions tour, Wilkinson said, 'It's like achieving a lifelong goal really. It's certainly not to be taken for granted'.

it's been very helpful. Finding time to pop out every now and again, to sit in a hotel room and watch TV, or chat to some of the guys about something other than rugby is great for me. It does the job of keeping me enthusiastic about training and playing.'

Wilkinson is also quick to pay tribute to the thousands of fans who travelled from Britain and Ireland to support the Lions. 'It's outstanding to run out in front of a crowd and see so much red in a place where you expect to see a lot of gold. It gives the Lions a huge boost on tour and I hope people realise how much they are doing in terms of backing us and pushing us forward to hopefully achieving our final goal.'

REACH FOR THE BEST

It's rare to find a recruitment consultancy who tackle personnel requirements with such tenacity and unfailing dedication. An unrivalled approach that has enabled Pertemps to remain unchallenged at the top of the league as the UK's leading independent recruitment consultancy.

As market leaders, we have developed our reputation not just by "filling positions" but by adding value to our client portfolio, a philosophy which is reflected in the diverse range of leading blue-chip companies that currently utilise our services.

Operating in three service divisions: commercial and professional, industrial and driving and technical and executive, our fully integrated service ensures that we are able to deliver quality personnel with the right skills, in the right place at the right time.

So, if you are seeking to win the competition for business, make sure that you retain the competition for talent by choosing Pertemps, Britain's most successful independent recruitment consultancy.

PERTEMPS
recruitment partnership
....

HEAD OFFICE:
Meriden Hall, Main Road, Meriden,
Warwickshire CV7 7PT.
Tel: 01676 525000 Fax: 01676 525009
Email: info@pertemps.co.uk
Web Site: www.pertemps.co.uk

The media was full of speculation about players being unhappy on tour, and Matt Dawson went as far as expressing his feelings in his newspaper column, but Wilkinson maintained after the first Test that he would not change anything about his first Lions experience. 'I've thoroughly enjoyed my time on tour so far, and it's been a truly memorable experience. I've learned a lot in the six weeks in Australia and I wouldn't have missed it for the world. It will be another four years before the next Lions trip, so I count myself very privileged to have been part of the 2001 Lions.'

At such a young age, Wilkinson still has a great deal to look forward to, and there is a lot more he wants to achieve. His ambition and determination are likely to bring him to New Zealand with the Lions in 2005, and he'll only be 30 when the Lions take on South Africa in 2009, so there's the possibility of two more tours. 'Its been a brilliant experience, and it's just a fantastic feeling to have so many successful individuals around you. It will certainly spur me on to achieve as much success as possible in the Six Nations, World Cups and future Lions tours. Basically, the aim must be to try to become the best in the world at what you do, and Lions tours are an important part of the overall picture. It'll take a lot of time, but Ill try not to let any chances go by.'

Wilkinson slips the Wallaby defensive net to score for the Lions just after half-time in the third and final Test at Sydney. Despite the fly half's 18 points in the match, victory remained out of reach for Wilkinson and the Lions. Perhaps next time… ?

WORLD CUP SEVENS IN ARGENTINA

BY IAN ROBERTSON

London Irish wing Paul Sackey on the attack for England against Spain at Mar del Plata. England lost this pool game 12-14 but still qualified for the main competition quarter-finals, in which they were defeated by eventual tournament runners-up Australia.

Argentina may not have been the obvious choice of venue for the third World Sevens tournament, but the International Rugby Board are right to take the sevens to places which would never expect to host the full 15-a-side World Cup. The first World Sevens was held in Scotland at Murrayfield in 1993, and as the game of sevens was conceived in the Borders of Scotland over a century ago this was a logical choice. The second World Sevens was held in 1997 in Hong Kong, and as the colony had hosted the biggest and best sevens competition every year in the preceding 20 years this decision was also greeted with general approval.

Argentina is unquestionably a country fully capable of hosting a major sporting occasion as they have proved with the soccer World Cup. Indeed soccer is the number one sport in the country, although the Argentinians have a long and distinguished tradition in rugby union. And so it was that in the last week of January all rugby roads led to the Mundialista Stadium in Mar del Plata.

Scotland had managed to find a couple of unexpected banana skins in the qualifying stages and they failed to win a place among the 24 countries competing in Argentina. All the other major rugby-playing countries made it to Mar del Plata, along with representatives from the emerging nations, who had spent the previous 12 months qualifying. The biggest disappointment of the Sevens World Cup was the lack of famous names in the teams from England, Wales, Ireland and France. With the domestic season in full swing and the start of the Six Nations Championship scheduled for the following weekend, it was inevitable that the top international players would not be available to travel to Argentina. This really sad state of affairs guaranteed the Melrose Cup would be a showdown between the giants of the southern hemisphere – New Zealand, Australia and sevens specialists Fiji.

To be fair, it has to be said that England did as well as they could have expected. They defied the odds which were stacked against them – lack of preparation, lack of competition in the build-up and the fact that no player from the full England squad was available for selection. In these circumstances they emerged from the tournament with their reputation greatly enhanced. In their pool matches they enjoyed wins over Chile, Zimbabwe and Japan but suffered an unexpected loss to Spain as well as an anticipated defeat against the cup favourites, New Zealand. It should be noted that England gave New Zealand their toughest game of the whole tournament, only losing 17-7, which was the All Blacks' narrowest win over the three days of competition. England alone of the

Russia's Vitali Sorokine with the Plate after his side's 24-12 victory over neighbours Georgia in the final.

European teams reached the quarter-finals of the main competition. They lost to Australia but were certainly not disgraced.

Wales suffered like England from selection restrictions, with all their most famous players back at home preparing for the Six Nations. The utter lunacy of playing the tournament that last weekend in January was blindingly obvious for everyone bar the organisers and administrators to see. It rendered the Home Unions virtually impotent and it made their 7,000-mile journey a lost cause before their plane had left the tarmac at Heathrow. Wales were drawn in Pool D and they managed to win just two matches. They beat America and Hong Kong but only drew with Portugal and lost to both Australia and Samoa. They qualified not for the main competition, the Melrose Cup, but for the Plate. In the quarter-finals they beat Japan before losing to Georgia in the semi-finals.

The Irish found the going even tougher in Pool A. Their sole success was a victory over Kenya. They drew with Korea and lost to Fiji, Argentina and Russia. That record relegated them to the Bowl competition, where they enjoyed a narrow win over Chinese Taipei in the quarter-finals, followed by a hefty defeat from Portugal in the semi-finals.

The less said about France the better. In Pool B they beat Taipei and Canada but lost to

South Africa, Georgia and Cook Islands. In the quarter-finals of the Bowl they lost to Kenya. The Bowl was won by Chile, who beat Portugal in the final. The Plate final turned out to be a local derby performed 6,000 miles from home – Russia beat Georgia.

As for the Melrose Cup, New Zealand reached the final with wins over Samoa in the quarter-finals and host nation Argentina in the semi-finals. From the other half of the draw, Australia followed up their win over England by beating Fiji in the semi-finals.

In the final, New Zealand ran out comfortable winners over Australia, and that was hardly a surprise. New Zealand took the World Sevens seriously. They picked a frighteningly strong squad and prepared with typical All Black ruthless efficiency. Over the weekend, in eight matches they scored 282 points, including 44 tries. They had the unstoppable Jonah Lomu to strike fear into the hearts of every one of his opponents. They had the best sevens forward of the last 20 years in Eric Rush, who was unfortunately injured and unable to play on the final day. They were awesome, and it was worth the journey to Argentina just to watch them. It was a good weekend, but of course it would have been so much better if all the best players in the world had been available for selection.

If there is to be a fourth World Sevens in 2005, then let us hope the organisers can choose a sensible date which allows every country to pick their best team. That, surely, has to be the whole point of any World Cup.

The ever-menacing Jonah Lomu takes on the Australians in the final of the Melrose Cup, the main competition. He scored three tries in the All Blacks' 31-12 victory.

A DECADE AT THE TOP:
John Eales

BY **RAECHELLE EDWARDS**

August 5, 2000. A cold, crisp day in windy Wellington on the South Island of New Zealand, and the All Blacks are leading the Wallabies 23-21 in another epic trans-Tasman encounter. Australia need victory in this match to keep the Bledisloe Cup and to maintain their hopes for Tri-Nations glory for the first time. On full-time, Australia are awarded a penalty in the All Blacks quarter. With regular kicker Stirling Mortlock off the field, the fate of the Wallabies rests on the shoulders of one man, John Eales. With a not-so-easy angle and the pressure of a nation, as well as 50,000 screaming Kiwis, Eales slots the goal and punches both arms into the air triumphantly as his team-mates flock to him. The Wallaby skipper is a hero again.

But that's just another day in the office for John Anthony Eales. 'The last thing I wanted to do was let the team down,' he says of that moment. And this dignity and poise epitomises the man they call 'Nobody' (because Nobody's perfect). Eales is the Superman of the Wallabies: a first-rate goal-kicker, an excellent scrummager, a phenomenal line-out jumper; he also has outstanding mobility and fine ball-handling skills. But above all, he leads – and he leads by example.

Eales has been through a lot in his decade at the top of international rugby. From spectacular victories to crippling injuries and the transition from amateurism to professionalism. And he has taken it all in his giant stride. His huge frame of two metres and 119 kilograms towers above most, but his size, coupled with athleticism, has made him the most complete lock in world rugby, consistently. And he has earned a place in history as Australia's most-capped captain.

In a career of countless highlights, for Eales, beating the British & Irish Lions in the three-match Test series in Australia in 2001 was exceptional. He has won every major trophy and

SUPPORTING TOWN HOUSES, COUNTRY HOUSES & BRICK HOUSES.

Cheltenham & Gloucester

www.cheltglos.co.uk

Cheltenham & Gloucester plc   Registered in England No. 2299428
Registered Office Barnett Way Gloucester GL4 3RL

series rugby has to offer. 'England is a team as good as any in the world, and when you add in the best from the other three countries, it makes for a pretty formidable outfit. The win was very satisfying for us, particularly to come from one-nil down in the series,' Eales commented. 'The series win said a lot about the quality of our team, from every player in the team to the management – it was a great effort from start to finish.

'It was a very significant win and the best thing about it was that almost all of our other major wins, the Tri-Nations, Bledisloe Cups and World Cups, have been away from home. This was the first time we could have an ultimate game and ultimate series in Australia in front of a home-town crowd,' he said. 'I think it was extra-special that the rugby-following public at home could enjoy the experience with the team on a first-hand basis.'

Eales has a no-fuss leadership style. He relies on the respect of team-mates and opposition as he leads from the front. 'Your reputation is on the line every time you run onto the field. If you don't perform, you lose face with the team and that hurts more than anything,' said Eales.

Hailing from a Queensland family with Italian heritage, Eales was a talented sportsman from a young age, excelling in athletics, basketball, cricket and rugby while at school at Marist Brothers College, Ashgove.

Eales won the best and fairest award in Brisbane club rugby in 1990 and made his debut for Queensland that year. He won his first cap for Australia at 21 years of age against Wales, just ahead of the Wallabies' 1991 World Cup campaign. He played in every match along the way to Australia's famous victory at Twickenham. His line-out

Above: Eales the line-out jumper snaffling ball against England at Twickenham in the 1991 World Cup final, won by Australia 12-6. Page 81: Eales the goal-kicker, against France in Paris in November 1998. The Wallabies won this game 32-21.

A second World Cup victory, and this time as captain. Eales is at the centre of things as the final whistle blows at the Millennium Stadium, Cardiff, bringing the final of RWC 99 to an end.

supremacy throughout this campaign earned Eales international recognition and a spot in the World XV team in 1992 in the Centenary series against the All Blacks.

'Two years before I was picked [for the Wallabies] I would never have thought I would play for Australia. When I first started, I had no expectations of what the end of the road would be like, or what the road along the way would be like, but I have certainly been thrilled and gracious for the opportunities I have had.'

Like most rugby players exposed at the highest level, Eales has suffered his share of injuries in his ten years playing international rugby, including a shoulder injury, which forced him to miss the entire 1993 season. He returned in the 1994 season and won his 50th cap against England at Twickenham in 1997. In the lead-up to the 1999 World Cup Eales missed the entire Super-12 and domestic Test season, again with a shoulder injury, but recovered in time to lead the Wallabies to their second William Webb Ellis Trophy. An Achilles injury kept Eales out of the Super-12 in 2001, but persistence and determination saw him take his team to a satisfying series win over the Lions for the first time in 102 years.

Eales hoists the Tom Richards Cup after the Wallaby series victory over the 2001 Lions.

Throughout his rugby career Eales experienced the transition from the amateur game to professionalism and says of it, 'I know I'm not alone when I say I'd still play rugby if there was no money in it.' Eales credits his team-mates with inspiring him to achieve so much in the game. When asked who has been his greatest foe, Eales refuses to pick out an individual, instead saying, 'Over all the years, New Zealand has consistently been the most difficult opponent.'

Eales has been a role model to young Australians and young rugby players the world over with his gracious and humble nature, his commitment as an ambassador of the game and his attitude as a sportsman. In 1999 he was awarded the Order of Australia (AM) for services to the community and rugby.

Beyond the rugby field, Eales plans a new career in retirement. 'I suppose you go to where your interests are and one of my main interests in recent times has been in the finance sector, so I'd like to maybe head in that way. I think the lessons in life I have learned along the way will help, Eales commented. 'I will stay involved in rugby in some way but I'm not sure how yet,' he added.

John and his wife Lara have two children, Elijah, who is three, and Sophia, who is one. 'Becoming a father has changed my life in such a positive way. Rugby has always been one of the most important parts of my life, it has been my chosen career and profession, so it has always been high on the list of priorities, but you've always got to keep your perspective, and family, I think, are always number one.'

ENGLAND IN NORTH AMERICA

BY **MARK SOUSTER**

It began inauspiciously amid a threatened boycott and a defeat by the Barbarians the day before departure but ended in triumph and a small but significant piece of history with that new English record of 11 consecutive international victories. That alone made England's three-week sortie in June to North America a success, but it remains but part of the story. Each of the five matches, which included three internationals (two against Canada and the third versus the United States), was won comfortably, players who will be the fulcrum of the side after the 2003 World Cup – if not before – emerged, while others fell out of contention, their star unlikely to shine again. New coaches and players were blooded seamlessly, proof that the system put in place by Clive Woodward is producing positive results.

Before departure, Woodward maintained it would be wrong to label the trip developmental, but by its very nature it was at least experimental. The absence of 18 Lions, increased to 19 with Martin Corry's departure for Australia, made it so. For the

Leicester flanker Lewis Moody, the player of the tour, gets away from Dan Lyle as England beat the United States 48-19 to record their eleventh straight international victory.

only time this year it provided Woodward and Brian Ashton, his able lieutenant, with the opportunity to assess the quality of the tier below senior level, to discover at first hand over a month who could make the grade and who might not. Additional assistant coaches were also exposed to the system, including John Wells, Ellery Hanley, Paul Grayson and Ged Glynn. Wells, whom the players held in the highest regard for his keen analytical rugby brain and quiet authority, made a particular impression.

In the meantime competition for places for the rearranged Six Nations game against Ireland will be intense. 'I am not anticipating anyone telling me they don't want to be part of what I am building, so the objective for the players on the tour was to try and break into that squad,' Woodward said. At least two should be involved in the 22 against the Irish, although Woodward, who was also impressed by the return of Graham Rowntree and Simon Shaw to the international arena, would not divulge their identity. But Lawrence Dallaglio's year-long absence following knee surgery will open doors.

Several individuals returned home with reputations enhanced. Among those mentioned in despatches were Ben Kay and Lewis Moody, the player of the tour. The Leicester duo were among 11 players capped against Canada and the United States, a total that included Jamie Noon, who adapted well to the unfamiliar inside-centre role, Michael Stephenson, who proved wrong critics of his defence, and Olly Barkley, the 19-year-old Bath prodigy. Barkley surely has a golden future ahead of him. He was capped before playing a first-class game for Bath, and has remarkable composure, mental strength and skill. He is a slightly stockier version of Jonny Wilkinson and even kicks left-footed. Above all, he always appeared to have that priceless ability enjoyed by few to find extra time and space. While fly half is his current position, do not rule out a move to inside centre in the long term. Wherever he plays, Barkley's is a name to remember. Then there was Josh Lewsey, the dynamic Wasps full back, who scored four tries on the tour and who Woodward feels would happily fill some of the 'big shoes' in the senior XV.

'Competition for places has to be healthy for England,' Kyran Bracken, the tour captain, said. 'People like Mike Catt and Will Greenwood need to know there are other players capable of coming into the side and taking their place. When I first came into the side there wasn't enough pressure being put on the established men. You can hardly say the same thing now. Barkley is just the latest in a long list who have come through on this tour alone. He has already shown immense composure and when you talk to him you don't feel as though you are speaking to such a young man.' Bracken, who forged a close relationship with Woodward, could even be the beneficiary of any backlash against Matt Dawson. Whatever the merits of the Northampton scrum half's outburst on the Lions tour to Australia, Woodward has never been impressed by loose tongues speaking out of turn. Richard Cockerill did so once in a book and has never been heard of again.

Moody's position is the most interesting. He will find it difficult to return to Welford Road and play third fiddle to Josh Kronfeld and Neil Back. Wells insists he will benefit

Former rugby league star Ellery Hanley conducts an England training session at the University of California, Berkeley. Hanley was one of several assistant coaches on tour.

Rising star Olly Barkley dummies an inside pass as the England tourists crush USA 'A' 83-21 at UCLA. Barkley was capped for England before playing a first-class game for his club, Bath.

ultimately by learning from the two masters, who themselves should be looking at the threat posed by Moody. While reluctant to leave Leicester, where he still has a two-year contract, he will be unhappy not to be given the opportunity to build on his advancement.

Success has raised a different dilemma – principally how to keep everyone happy when expectations have been raised. Ideally Woodward would like to raise the profile and status of the 'A' team, install full-time management and even consider dual tours to beef up the fixture list. The majority of the party who toured North America could well be

heading to the other side of the Pacific in 12 months' time. 'It is my gut feeling that when we go to Fiji, Samoa and Tonga next year, we will be letting a lot of our top players have a summer off,' Woodward said. 'We need to recognise how important the 'A' team is.' With a World Cup on the horizon, Woodward at least knows that the locker is full. He has talent at his disposal that other countries can only envy. Making the most of it has been England's perennial problem. But under Woodward, the omens look distinctly bright. The young guns are ready to make their mark.

THE RUGBY TOUR IN THE 21ST CENTURY: Solihull School to Canada

BY **S.A. MORGAN** WITH INTRODUCTION BY **IAN ROBERTSON**

The annual rugby tour has changed out of all recognition since I was at school in the far-off days of black-and-white television. In the middle of the last century, schools had a few away matches with the occasional stopover, but all within the UK.

In recent years the world has shrunk. Over 20,000 supporters flew to Australia to follow the Lions. Now the progressive schools are also branching out. I know of a dozen schools in the past three years who have gone to New Zealand, South Africa, Australia, Argentina, the Far East and America.

Last year I attended a dinner to help Solihull School raise funds for the 1st XV squad to go to Canada. This was just one event in a whole series of fund-raising activities, which the boys pursued in the 12 months leading up to the trip of a lifetime. There is no doubt this is a rapidly growing industry, and the wonderful, unforgettable experiences which the Solihull boys enjoyed in Canada will be shared by a growing number of schoolboys in the future. The report from their master in charge of rugby should certainly whet the appetites of a lot of school 1st XVs.

Ian Robertson

Early in the morning of 12 August 2000, 23 pupils, three staff and our doctor left Birmingham airport bound for Toronto. We were about to embark upon an action-packed, five-match rugby tour of eastern Canada. Our itinerary allowed us to experience the major cities – Toronto, Ottawa and Montreal – while also providing us with the opportunity to sample Canada's 'great outdoors'. Our accommodation was a perfect mix of hotel, university and billeting. When not playing or indeed training for rugby, we certainly experienced the full spectrum of leisure and recreational opportunities.

After a morning training session, an excursion to Wonderland (Canada's answer to Disneyland) was followed by a ride on the Peterborough Lift-lock and a trip to an authentic Indian reserve. We then played our first game, against Peterborough, on the waterfront at Beavermead Park. It was a magnificent performance, with all 23 Solihull players taking the field (the heat made it essential), the final score being 62-3.

Our next port of call was a place called Deep River in the Upper Ottawa Valley. We were welcomed by an informal beach party at which the club members vowed to look after us for the whole of the next day, right up to our 7 p.m. fixture. Little did we know this would include sailing across to Quebec and hiking up the infamous Mount Martin! Despite this pre-match preparation, we again turned on the style to record an astounding 58-3 victory. The evening culminated in an excellent barbecue dinner at the local Yacht and Tennis club. Quite a day! By way of carrying on the outdoor feel, we spent our next day (17 August) white-water rafting – an amazing experience thoroughly enjoyed by all.

Next stop was Montreal and our fixture against Sainte-Anne-De-Bellevue RFC – a very tough physical encounter, which tested our discipline and cohesion to the full. The outcome was a 35-0 win. Relaxation time in Montreal after the previous evening's match was spent on a jetboat ride down the Lachine Rapids, with a trip to the city's Imax cinema and Science Center in the afternoon.

Our next fixture, against Ottawa Scottish, was played at Twin Elm Park, one of Canadian rugby's national stadiums. Against a very experienced side, we again kept our nerve to retain our unbeaten record, winning 26-0.

Now on the last leg of our tour, we headed back to Toronto to meet our final set of hosts and opponents, Ajax Wanderers. Yet again, the hospitality was fabulous, and the opposition provided us with our stiffest test yet. The squad responded with our fifth and certainly most pleasing victory, 26-11.

Before departing for Toronto airport, we did leave ourselves with a couple of days to do some final sightseeing and make some last visits. Our collective journey up the CN Tower was certainly memorable, not least because when we were at the top the roof of the Sky Dome stadium retracted so we could just about make out the players of the Toronto Blue Jays and Kansas City Royals warming up for a game we were about to take our seats for! We had a great time at the baseball, the home team won and the atmosphere was brilliant.

To ensure we missed nothing out, we spent the day before departure at Niagara, taking the Maid of the Mist boat journey and the Journey Behind the Falls tour to the Table Rock vantage point. We certainly enjoyed an incredibly memorable tour, experiencing everything that Canadian life and hospitality had to offer and, most importantly, winning all of our fixtures in fine style.

The Solihull School tour party to Canada, August 2000.

RACE WIDE OPEN FOR WRWC 2002

BY **CHRIS THAU**

Rebuilding and consolidation are the key words in the women's game as the leading teams fine-tune their preparations for the Women's Rugby World Cup 2002 in Barcelona. The fast-approaching second official WRWC is helping to concentrate the minds of both players and coaches. The England captain's logbook during last summer's tour to New Zealand and Australia is illuminating in this respect. Before the second Test against New Zealand, Paula George wrote: 'There is only one true thing that matters for both teams. Who will lift the 2002 World Cup in Barcelona?' Well, genuine evidence is emerging that some of the leading teams are catching up with the formidable Black Ferns, who were, until July 2001, undefeated for a decade.

Last February, the first ever Women's Six Nations Championship kicked off, with Ireland returning to the fold after a two-year break. The foot-and-mouth crisis disrupted the proceedings, with some of the Irish fixtures being cancelled rather than postponed. England, buoyed by the appointment of former Wallaby full back Geoff Richards as their first full-time coach, won their fixtures with comparative ease.

During the championship, England showed glimpses of the potential fully displayed during the tour to Australia and New Zealand, arguably the most significant undertaking in their build-up for WRWC 2002. During their tour Down Under, the English won both Australian Tests – 41-19 and 15-5 – and arrived in New Zealand full of confidence. Defeated 15-10 by the Black Ferns in the first Test, the English displayed remarkable self-belief and resolve to bounce back in the second, to win 22-17 after an epic battle and share the series. The English win in New Zealand, coupled with Canada's unexpected but equally impressive 23-3 win over the US Eagles, admittedly rebuilding for 2002, has added spice to the already exciting race for the Holy Grail of women's rugby.

Between the Six Nations and the tour of Australia and New Zealand, the English, helped by a substantial National Lottery grant, had gathered their senior squad for a week-long camp and sent their development team to the annual European Championship, the biggest international women's competition after the WRWC and held this year in the northern French rugby stronghold of Lille. The top seven European teams – France, the 2000 champions; Spain, last year's beaten finalists; England, the 2001 Six Nations champions; plus Scotland, Ireland, Wales, Italy and the guests from Asia, Kazakhstan, competed in the first division. Sweden, Belgium, Germany and the Netherlands made up the second division. Their success the previous year had somewhat lulled France into a sense of false confidence and they paid dearly for it. Not only did they lose in the semi-finals – admittedly by one score to the eventual winners Scotland – but they also suffered the indignity of being beaten during the tournament by the second string English XV, strengthened by two experienced players: veteran scrum half Emma Mitchell and hooker and forwards leader Nicky Ponsford.

'The match against Scotland was the worst performance by a French national team in living memory,' said Wanda Noury, the chairperson of the FFR Women's Commission. Ms Noury, a former referee, who represents the women's game on the FRR Board,

pointed out that development is high on the priority list of the French Federation and that the women's national team will be subject to an injection of youth in the build-up to WRWC 2002. There is very little doubt that the French, though competitive and inventive, seemed unable to compete on equal terms with the abrasive and dynamic English. Some of the veterans seemed off the pace as the fast-flowing encounter entered the final stages. Even the dependable Natalie Amiel, the French playmaker, appeared out of sorts – not to mention position, as she was playing at centre and also threw into the line out on the French ball.

Sweden test the Netherlands defence during the second division clash in the 2001 European Championship, held at Lille.

The Welsh, coached by former Abertillery and Ebbw Vale No. 8 John Williams and under a new captain, fly half Rhian Williams, had made considerable progress in the months leading up to the tournament and in the first round gave Scotland one of their hardest games in recent memory. 'It was more of a case us losing it, rather than Scotland winning it. We made two defensive errors and then failed to score with the line begging, a couple of times… The rest was very much on par… But, that's life. It will only help us in the long term. I hope we will be able to do ourselves justice next year in Barcelona,' said Williams.

This was Rhian Williams's first match as skipper, the 22-year-old Imperial College medical student having inherited the captaincy from 37-year-old No. 8 Lisa Burgess, who is in her final season of international rugby. Burgess, a schoolteacher in Bristol, is one of the legends of the women's game, having played in 1986 for Great Britain against France

Skippers of Wales past and present. Rhian Williams (right) led Wales in the European Championship, having inherited the captaincy from Lisa Burgess (left). Opposite top: Spain get the ball away against Scotland in the championship final. Opposite bottom: Scotland, winners of the 2001 European Championship. Player of the tournament Paula Chalmers is second from left in the front row, while skipper 'Jock' Findlay holds the trophy.

in the first ever women's international played on British soil, and she has given the young fly half her full and unconditional support.

Speaking after the bruising encounter against Kazakhstan, which saw Wales retain their fifth place in Europe, Burgess said: 'Although a bit emotional, with the WRWC around the corner, this transfer had to take place sooner rather than later. I have been around for a while and this was my 60th cap for Wales. I have been around since the days women's rugby was more of a social game, but we have made huge strides forward in a very short time.

'The game is more athletic, much faster and more physical than it was 15 years ago when I started. I belong to a fortunate generation of Loughborough University graduates, who learned the game from one of the finest coaches and teachers of the game – Jim Greenwood. We have a tremendous structure in Wales – Under 14, Under 15, Under 17 and Under 19 – managed by the WRU director for women's rugby, Richard Hodges, and a lot of talent is coming through. Rhian is a fine player and a superb leader. Simply, they could have not chosen a better captain and I shall endeavour to give her my full support until I leave the national team, which hopefully will be after next year's World Cup.'

The Scots, with playmaker and scrum half Paula Chalmers in superb form, defeated Spain 15-3 in the final to win the coveted trophy and secure themselves a fine position in the seedings for next year's WRWC tournament. The Scots, marshalled by their tireless captain, Karen 'Jock' Findlay, managed to absorb the early Spanish pressure and struck back with two well-taken tries – one in each half – to deflate the never-say-die Spanish ladies. Chalmers – the sister of the Scotland and British Lions outside half Craig Chalmers – and skipper Findlay gave credit for Scotland's outstanding performance to the work of the coaching team, led by Peter Brownlie.

Chalmers, winner of the player of the tournament award, felt that the emotion in the aftermath of Scotland's first ever win against the French on their home ground must have accounted for their unusually high level of concentration in the final. 'This has been a massive day for the team and Scottish rugby. We had won the Five Nations before, but we had never won three matches in a week, which should put us in good stead for next year in Barcelona. We were so overwrought by the win against France, and I have to say that it was a very hard match in Armentières, that we had no time to be nervous for the final. As far as the trophy is concerned, I am totally gobsmacked, simply because I do not believe we, as a team, played as well as we could, and I, personally, have not played particularly well. But then we won, and we will celebrate.'

The Old Monk
COMPANY

Incorporating

Drinking a toast to the
Wooden Spoon Society.

THE FIFTH RUGBY WORLD CUP KICKS OFF

BY **CHRIS THAU**

Malta's scrum half, Kevin Davidson, comes under pressure from the Moldovan pack during the Mediterranean island's 58-8 defeat in Pool One.

The irresistible attraction of the Rugby World Cup is emphasised by the fortunes of a 45-year-old Welshman, Ray Watts, who turned up to play for Malta in the qualifying rounds of RWC 2003. Qualified for Malta through his mother Doris, Watts was selected for the match against Monaco, the second international of the newly formed team.

The RWC debut of the Maltese team, which Watts had missed, was a moderate disaster, with Malta finishing at the wrong end of a 58-8 drubbing at the hands of the hard men of Moldova. Malta, one of the newest IRB members, had embarked on an energetic player-recruitment programme to strengthen their squad for their matches against Moldova, Monaco, Belgium, Lithuania and Slovenia in Pool One of the first round of the European qualifiers for 2003.

Europe, with 32 entries and four qualifying slots in the 2003 finals, is the largest of the five RWC qualifying zones and commenced playing in September 2000, when Norway hosted Luxembourg in the first match of the fifth RWC competition. The first rounds involved 18 teams playing in what is called the European Nations Bowl section – the FIRA-AER third division in all but name – divided into three pools of six.

Due to the harsh Continental winter, the qualifying process was halted in November 2000, with Belgium and Moldova in Pool One, Switzerland in Pool Two and Sweden and

Latvia in Pool Three leading the tables undefeated. The 45-match first round marathon, which resumed action in March, ended in June, with four of the five winter pool table leaders – Belgium, Switzerland, Sweden and Latvia (as the fourth-best team) – qualifying for Round Two. Needless to say, Malta failed to win any of their matches, but the team, coached by New Zealander Len Ethell, is wiser and delighted with the experience.

Belgium finished the pool unbeaten, leaving Slovenia and Moldova, in that order, in their trail, and will play in Pool Two of the second European qualifying round alongside FIRA-AER second division (Plate) regulars Ukraine, Croatia and Czech Republic and fellow qualifiers Switzerland – winners of Pool Two, Round One. The Swiss, coached by Yan Braendlin and Regis Tabarini, targeted the match against Andorra in May as key to their qualifying ambitions.

Indeed, the seven-try, 38-25 thriller in Lausanne secured Switzerland the pole position in their pool, though a somewhat disjointed performance saw them go down 13-10 to Yugoslavia. Meanwhile, the Serbs experienced a most frustrating campaign, wrecked by their 23-13 defeat at the hands of Bosnia. Andorra's hopes of reaching the second round were effectively dashed by the lively Hungarians, who, with full back Miklos Dobai scoring a hat-trick of tries, defeated their visitors 27-21 in October last year.

Above: Maltese international Ray Watts and admirers.
Right: The Hungarian team in a pre-match huddle. The Hungarians proved too hot for Andorra but could manage no higher than third in Pool Two.

In Pool Three Sweden, coached by a team co-ordinated by Scotland's Guy Deanwoody, finished top of the table, with Latvia in the runners-up position. Israel, who started their campaign with a 62-3 thumping of Luxembourg, were a disappointment, losing 6-21 at home to Austria, a defeat which effectively ended their campaign. The Swedes, whose 116-3 defeat of Luxembourg is the highest score of the competition so far, confirmed their credentials with a hard-earned 17-10 win against Latvia in the final match of the pool. However, the Latvians, who had both the ability and the personnel to upset the smooth progression of the Swedes, manage to qualify for Round Two as the fourth-best team, joining Sweden and European second division powers Poland, Denmark and Germany in the second pool of the European zone.

Round Two, which kicked off in September 2001, therefore involved ten nations: the four qualifiers – Belgium, Switzerland, Sweden and Latvia – plus the six FIRA-AER Plate teams: Poland, Czech Republic, Ukraine, Croatia, Denmark and Germany. The two Round Two pool winners qualify for Round Three, where they join the bottom four teams of the six nations (Romania, Georgia, Spain, Portugal, Russia and Netherlands) playing in the European Nations Cup. The six nations in Round Three compete for two slots in the fourth and final act of the European qualifying saga, to be played between September and November 2002. The six teams taking part in Round Four are Ireland, Italy, the winners and runners-up of the European Nations Cup and the two Round Three pool winners. Four of the six teams involved in Round Four qualify for the RWC 2003 finals. The remaining two take part in two play-off matches, home and away, to determine who plays in the Repechage against those in a similar position from Asia, Africa, Americas and Oceania.

Belgian lock Alain Magnier in full stride. The Belgians finished unbeaten in Round One, Pool One and passed into Round Two, Pool Two, along with Switzerland, winners of Round One, Pool Two.

The Oceania qualifying zone was the next to kick off last June, with a series of matches between Cook Islands, Tahiti and the island of Niue in the Eastern Section, and Papua New Guinea, Vanuatu and Solomon Islands in the Western. Cook Islands and Papua New Guinea won their respective sections; Solomon Islands, Niue, and Vanuatu were making their debut in the main RWC competition. Cook Islands started with a 14-try, 86-0 demolition of Tahiti, in which Lance Fitzpatrick scored eight tries, the second-highest individual match tally in international rugby. (The record is held by Hong Kong's Ashley Billington, with ten tries in Hong Kong's 164-13 annihilation of Singapore in 1994.) A laboured 29-10 win over Niue saw Cook Islands through to the second round, along with Papua New Guinea, who recorded identical scores of 32-10 against Solomon Islands at home in Port Moresby and against Vanuatu in Port Vila. In the next round, the two take on the might of the Pacific, with Samoa, Tonga and Fiji entering the fray.

The African zone started in July, with the game between RWC 'veterans' Zambia, making their second appearance in RWC qualifiers, and newcomers Cameroon, making their international debut. The winner of this three-nation pool is likely to be determined by the clash between Zambia and another RWC newcomer, Uganda, with the former having the advantage of experience, despite playing away from home in Kampala. In the other pool, an intriguing contest pitches Botswana against Swaziland and the mystery men from Madagascar, with the clash between Botswana and Madagascar in Antananarivo likely to decide the outcome of the pool. The two pool winners qualify for Round Two, which also involves Kenya.

The first round of the Americas zone will conclude sometime in October 2001. One of the pools comprises Bahamas, Barbados, Bermuda, Cayman Islands, Guyana, Jamaica, St Lucia, Trinidad and Tobago, while the other contains Brazil, Columbia, Peru and Venezuela. The two pool winners play home and away for a place in the next round, where Chile and Paraguay await.

Finally, in Asia the format has been changed for the first time since 1991, with RWC deciding to abandon the system of using the Asian Tournament and a qualifying round. The first round of the competition will involve nine unions, the top three in the Asian Plate, the top three in the Asian Shield, the winners and the runners-up in the Asian Bowl plus Chinese Taipei. The winners of the three pools compete among themselves in Round Two, with the winner joining Japan and Korea for the final Asian round. The winners of Round Three go through to RWC 2003, while the runners-up enter the Repechage.

The draw for the 20-nation RWC 2003 finals, organised in four pools of five teams, was released late last year, with Australia, France, South Africa and New Zealand the top seeds of the fifth RWC tournament. Two pools will be hosted by New Zealand and two by Australia, with the top two teams in each pool progressing to the quarter-finals. The eight quarter-finalists of RWC 99 are qualified directly to the tournament finals, following a decision of the IRB Council. The 58-match competition hosted by the Australian Rugby Union will take place during October/November 2003, with the opening match and the final being played at Stadium Australia in Sydney.

Australian Rugby Union CEO John O'Neill has said that the Rugby World Cup is Australia's next big opportunity after the Olympics to demonstrate to the world its capacity to handle major international events. 'We are expecting more than 50,000 inbound tourists, and following the success of the Olympics, perhaps even more. The British Lions, who played ten matches, including Tests in Brisbane, Melbourne and Sydney, have provided an excellent dress rehearsal for the World Cup. We really want Australia to host the best Rugby World Cup ever.'

ARU RWC 2003 Management Team

Senior Advisor, Special Projects
Geoff Parmenter
Tournament Planning
Eddie Moore
Senior Manager Events & Operations
George Perry
Tournament Events & Operations
Ian Alker
Tournament Events Manager
Ben Einfeld
Licensing Co-ordinator
Jessica Hurford

RUGBY WORLD CUP 2003:
The route from Europe to Australia

ROUND ONE
European Nations Bowl: 18 teams in three pools of six

POOL ONE	POOL TWO	POOL THREE
Belgium	*Switzerland*	*Sweden*
Moldova	*Yugoslavia*	*Latvia*
Slovenia	*Hungary*	*Luxembourg*
Monaco	*Andorra*	*Austria*
Lithuania	*Bosnia*	*Norway*
Malta	*Bulgaria*	*Israel*

ROUND TWO
Ten teams in two pools of five, consisting of the three pool
winners and the best second-placed team from Round One
(marked with *) plus six European Nations Plate teams

POOL ONE	POOL TWO
*Sweden	**Belgium*
*Latvia	**Switzerland*
Germany	*Ukraine*
Poland	*Croatia*
Denmark	*Czech Republic*

ROUND THREE
Six teams in two pools of three, consisting of the two pool
winners from Round Two plus the teams placed third to sixth in
the European Nations Cup

ROUND FOUR
Six teams in two pools of three, consisting of Ireland and Italy
and the winners and runners-up of the European Nations Cup
plus the two pool winners from Round Three

AUSTRALIA 2003
Four teams qualify: the winners and runners-up from the two
pools in Round Four (the winners of a play-off between the two
third-placed teams pass to Repechage)

NEXT

ARE PROUD TO SUPPORT

THE WOODEN SPOON SOCIETY
RUGBY WORLD 2002

REVIEW OF
THE SEASON
2000-01

LLOYDS TSB SIX NATIONS CHAMPIONSHIP

BY **ALASTAIR HIGNELL**

England's rugby league convert Jason Robinson takes off on a typical jinking run against Scotland at Twickenham. The Sale Sharks wing was yet another cutting edge in an already exciting England set-up.

There may have been plenty of fireworks, notably from a rampant, record-breaking England, but the Lloyds TSB Six Nations Championship 2001 still ended up like a damp squib. Ireland couldn't fulfil three fixtures because of the foot-and-mouth epidemic. For the first time since 1967, and the last outbreak of the disease, the tournament had to be carried over into a new season.

England were left just one victory short of a Grand Slam, with only Ireland standing between them and a successful defence of their Six Nations title. To give themselves the chance of a winner-takes-all Grand Slam showdown, the Irish would have to win in both Cardiff and Edinburgh, before playing host to England at Lansdowne Road. Any slips along the way and England would be champions without having to win in Dublin.

While Clive Woodward and his men would be only too happy to hang on to the silverware, coming away empty-handed from Dublin is not an option they would care to contemplate. They need no reminding that in each of the last two seasons their final match was away from home with a Grand Slam at stake. In 1999 they lost to Wales at Wembley and handed the title to Scotland. In 2000 they lost to Scotland at Murrayfield.

From the way England began the 2001 season, it was obvious that they weren't so much keen on burying those memories as on obliterating them. They marched on Cardiff for a first ever match at the Millennium Stadium with four straight victories over southern hemisphere opposition behind them. After that April defeat in the mud and rain of Murrayfield they'd succumbed to South Africa in Pretoria only to bounce back to beat the Boks at Bloemfontein and Twickenham, with home victories over world champions Australia and the Pumas sandwiched in between.

Wales fancied their chances – especially at home. Welsh clubs had done well in the Heineken Cup, the autumn internationals had been encouraging and key players like Rob Howley, Neil Jenkins and Scott Quinnell were on form. But, as it soon became apparent, England had taken their game to a different level. Wales were in the match for all of two minutes, at which point a Scott Gibbs chip caught England full back Iain Balshaw in two minds and Dafydd James nearly nipped in for the try.

Will Greenwood dives in for one of his three tries against Wales at the Millennium Stadium. The Harlequins centre was part of a formidable England midfield partnership along with Bath's Mke Catt.

That was the cue for England to go into overdrive with some expansive, imaginative and brilliantly executed attacking rugby. By the half-hour they had scored three superb tries. At half-time they were 29-8 ahead and with a quarter of the match to go they had run in six tries, including a hat-trick for Will Greenwood and a pair for Matt Dawson.

That Wales kept England out thereafter was scant consolation, as were the individual brilliance of Howley – who created tries for himself and Quinnell – and the landmark reached by Jenkins, whose conversion of the last try took him past 1,000 points in international rugby. Wales were shell-shocked, England were rampant.

**CUT OUT
THIS
ARMBAND.
UNFORTUNATELY,
YOU MAY
NEED IT.**

One-in-thirteen men in Great Britain get prostate cancer. Don't be
a statistic. Call 0845 300 8383 or visit www.prostate-cancer.org.uk

THE
PROSTATE
CANCER
CHARITY

England's electric full back Iain Balshaw leaves Scotland's Alan Bulloch trailing during his devastating two-try display at Twickenham.

Back at Twickenham, against the luckless Italians, England were irresistible. The 80 points they ran in and the 57-point margin of victory were championship records, as was Jonny Wilkinson's personal haul of 35 points. As against Wales, there was plenty of room for improvement. The Italians scored the first of 12 tries in the match, were level at 20-all after half an hour and only 33-23 down at the break. But the floodgates burst open in the second half, England scoring 47 points without reply.

It was sublime stuff against fragile opposition, but would it work in Dublin against an also unbeaten Ireland? That question was put on hold as the IRFU bowed to the wishes of the Irish government and called off the late March showdown. England were left therefore with two more matches at fortress Twickenham – against a lacklustre Scotland and an unconvincing France. Both teams were put to the sword by record scores. Scotland were competitive for half an hour but conceded six tries, two of them to devastating full back Iain Balshaw. France actually led 16-13 at half-time, but they too leaked six tries, all of them converted by Jonny Wilkinson as he sailed past Rob Andrew's record as England's leading points scorer in Tests.

France and Italy had both played Ireland by the time foot-and-mouth took hold. As a result both completed their Six Nations campaigns on time. Neither were happy with the results. Italy inevitably suffered second season syndrome and were further exposed by the prolonged absence, through a mixture of suspension and injury, of playmaking half backs Alessandro Troncon and Diego Dominguez.

Mauro Bergamasco lays hold of England back-rower Joe Worsley. First capped at 19 and still in his early 20s, Bergamasco has already developed into one of the stars ot the Italian team.

Nevertheless, the Azzurri averaged over 20 points a match and gave each of their opponents, even England, a scare. In Mauro Bergamasco they had perhaps the outstanding open-side flanker in the competition, while prop Andrea Lo Cicero and centre Cristian Stoica were quickly targeted by Premiership clubs.

But in all their matches the Italians suffered from a lack of concentration, a lack of discipline, a lack of fitness, or a combination of all three. In their opening match, against Ireland in Rome, Italy were just 19-15 down at half-time, but in the period immediately after the break the defence went AWOL, Rob Henderson scored the second and third tries of his hat-trick, Shane Horgan also touched down, and Ireland were home and hosed. Against England, Italy were level at 20-all after half an hour yet, admittedly in the face of some imperious attacking play, threw in the defensive towel in the second half. Against France, they were in contention throughout the match without ever being in control. Even so, if Christophe Lamaison had not had such a poor day with the boot the margin of defeat would have been far greater than 30-19.

The match against Scotland at Murrayfield was effectively a wooden spoon decider. Both teams were searching for a first win. Scotland were seeking revenge for the previous season's humiliation in Rome. Italy firmly believed that lightning could strike twice. Once again they had a good first half, leading 10-6 at the break after Bergamasco had scored an outstanding try. Once again ill-discipline cost them dear as Duncan Hodge fired over five penalties and a dropped goal to edge Scotland home by 23 points to 19.

The final match, at home to Wales, summed up their season – plenty of honest endeavour, a good try from workhorse Carlo Checchinato, a near faultless kicking display from Dominguez but also a certain naivety in defence and a tendency to fall apart under pressure. For once they conceded early scores – Wales scrum half Gareth Cooper crossed for a debut try after seven minutes; Scott Gibbs touched down twice before three-quarters of an hour was up – and for once they finished strongly, but for once they were never really in with a chance of victory.

If the Italians had a right to be disappointed by their Six Nations showing, France deserved to be suicidal. The mitigating factors of the previous year – a horrendous run of injuries, a settling-in period with a new coach, post-World Cup hangover – no longer applied. Indeed, France went into the tournament on the back of a stunning win over the All Blacks in Marseilles. But their opening match at the Stade de France, a 16-6 win over Scotland, was uninspired and error-ridden, while their other game at their headquarters saw them hand a 45-33 victory to Wales despite dominating the first period of the match and regaining the lead with just five minutes to go.

Between those matches the French travelled to Ireland and started so badly that they were 22-3 down in less than an hour. A storming comeback was not enough. They lost 22-15. They beat the Italians in Rome but despite running in three tries to one still managed to look unconvincing and out of sorts.

The 'Pau Rocket', aka Philippe Bernat-Salles, is stopped in his tracks by Ireland's Rob Henderson as France succumb 22-15 at Lansdowne Road.

At least the French made some sort of a fight of it against England at Twickenham. But the way they folded after going into half-time 16-13 ahead, eventually losing 48-19, was enough to pose real questions about the future of coach Bernard Laporte and about the character of some of his players. A return of two wins from five matches was simply not good enough.

Wales and Scotland at least ended the season in better spirits than they began it. On the opening weekend of the tournament, the former were thrashed by England, while the latter could gain little consolation from defeat by France in Paris. The extraordinary 28-all draw between the two at Murrayfield therefore represented a bit of a bonus for both teams. Both ended their seasons with victory over Italy. In the meantime there was despair for the Scots at Twickenham, delight for the Welsh in Paris.

Tom Smith sets his sights on the Wales try line and nothing is going to stop him scoring Scotland's third try in the 28-28 draw at Murrayfield.

Both could still finish ahead of Ireland, whose 100 per cent record from two matches hinted at the emergence of a team to be reckoned with, without doing enough to confirm it. The Irish took their chances well against Italy in Rome and defended heroically against France in Dublin. In Keith Wood and Brian O'Driscoll they possess two of the outstanding players in the European game. With four other Irishmen also making the Lions tour party to Australia, and Munster again doing well in Europe, Ireland looked on the point of developing real strength in depth. The curtailment of the Six Nations meant that their case could not be proven either way.

THE CLUB SCENE

ENGLAND – A successful year in Europe

BY BILL MITCHELL

For English rugby the 2000-01 season was memorable for a number of reasons, not least being the fact that the national team won all its matches, while at club level English teams – Leicester and Harlequins respectively – brought home the two prestigious European trophies, the European Cup and Shield, having triumphed in competitions previously mostly dominated by French clubs.

In fact, Leicester can lay claim to being the outstanding northern hemisphere club without any argument, since they also won the English Zurich Premiership by an eight-point margin from runners-up Wasps and completed a treble by winning the Zurich Premiership play-off competition too, with a comprehensive 22-10 victory over Bath in the Twickenham final.

The only trophy available to them that was missing was the Tetley's Bitter Cup, and this was denied them by Harlequins, who won a thrilling semi-final at the Stoop Memorial Ground 22-18, before succumbing in the final at Twickenham to a Newcastle Falcons recovery, which produced an injury-time winning try by Dave Walder, which Jonny Wilkinson converted.

Leicester celebrate their success in the Zurich Premiership. The Zurich Championship and the Heineken European Cup were to follow, making it a memorable season for the Tigers.

This was cruel for the Quins, as they seemed to have established a winning 27-16 lead with only a few minutes left, while the winning try owed something to an apparent error by touch judge Lander, who awarded Newcastle a line-out throw on the Quins line, when all the evidence suggested that the defending team should have been given that advantage. Stuart Grimes's line-out catch led to the try.

But the Quins were not finished and subsequently won revenge in a European Shield semi-final against Newcastle, with stand-in fly half Craig Chalmers outstanding. They then went to the Madejski Stadium in Reading to take the honours with an extra-time success by 42 points to 33 against gallant Narbonne from France. For Harlequins it had been in many ways a traumatic season, which left them in the end lying one place from bottom in the Zurich Premiership. They gained a new boss in former Saracen Mike Evans, who took over from Zinzan Brooke early in the New Year. However, the European Shield success means entry to the new season's European Cup, so is all well that ends well?

An irony about the cup arrangements for the season just past was that what should have been the climax to the season – the Tetley's Bitter Cup final at Twickenham – was played on 24 February. This suggested that the top brass at RFU headquarters and/or the leading clubs themselves wanted to downgrade that competition and place the full emphasis for public acceptance on the Zurich Premiership play-offs at the end of the season. If that was the plan it scarcely worked out as plotted, since the February date – in cold weather – drew an attendance of 71,000, while the play-off final on the second Sunday in May attracted only 33,000 fans. Other sports have the national final as their climax, so have the powers that be now accepted the message? Or do they know better? Possibly, as the cup final will in 2002 be held on 20 April, while the Zurich Premiership big day will be in early June, by which time many will not only be thinking about their holidays but may indeed be on them.

The bottom place in the Premiership went to the unfortunate Rotherham, who have been one of the National League's success stories. Their outclassed position would suggest that the top clubs have a point when they oppose automatic promotion and relegation, but such a system is enshrined in most credible competitions, and ambitious clubs should never be denied the chance to play at the top level. An end-of-season play-off between the bottom Premiership side and top National League club would appear to be the logical answer to the problem.

Taking the Rotherham hot seat will be Leeds from National League Division One, Worcester being denied the honour late in the campaign by the narrowest of margins, but it was sad to see two famous clubs – Orrell and Waterloo – at the foot of the table and relegated. Further down, the foot-and-mouth problem meant that Division Two and Division Three North both ended with incomplete programmes, although the enterprising Bracknell and Stourbridge respectively did quite enough to rise to pastures new. Sedgley Park in Division Three North won a play-off against Launceston (Division Three South runners-up) for a place in Division Two, from which Camberley, Lydney and poor, pointless and once high-flying West Hartlepool sadly descend. Plymouth Albion (Division Three South champions) had an outstanding season in winning all their league matches, while it will be interesting to see how the newcomers from the regional competitions perform in better company. Old Colfeians (London), Scunthorpe (Midlands), Darlington Mowden Park (North) and Old Patesians (South West) carry with them the best wishes of all those who like to welcome new faces.

However, as far as promotion and relegation has been concerned, once again it would seem that the leagues' organisers have moved the goalposts during the season, and clubs

must remain confused about what their ultimate fates might be until the authorities make it clear that the rules that start a season will be rigorously and fairly applied at the end of it. In other sports changes during a campaign are always totally unacceptable and frequently lead to legal action.

Tom Palmer of Leeds Tykes is brought down by Northampton's Dan Richmond during the Tetley's Bitter Cup clash at Franklin's Gardens.

Even in these professional days other things of value still exist, and the Barbarians continue to thrive at a time when many see them as being irrelevant. They had seven outings in the latest season and won four of them, with a final flourish against Wales in Cardiff (40-38), Scotland at Murrayfield (74-31) and England's tourists to North America at Twickenham (43-29). As long as the game's leading players continue to look upon appearances for the club as being an honour, the Barbarians will continue to enthral people who enjoy open and uninhibited rugby and watching the likes of Jonah Lomu strut upon the stage. Tradition does still matter in sport.

In another strong burst Oxford University centre Werner van Pittius hands off Cambridge fly half Simon Amor.

In a similar way the Varsity Match at Twickenham continues to attract crowds of over 50,000 and thus contradicts those media cynics who consider the event to be 'over-hyped'. A good Oxford retained the Bowring Bowl by beating a gallant Cambridge side, which led until near the end in a fine game before the wing Jennings was sent away by the immense centre Werner van Pittius to score his and the Dark Blues' second try. The previously admirable and accurate Simon Amor at fly half for the Light Blues had a chance to earn his side a draw, but his late penalty drifted wide. The conditions were awful, but the fare was superb.

The BUSA title was won for the first time by Exeter University, who scored the same number of points (24) as Northumbria in a Twickenham thriller but took the trophy on a better try count. The Army's grip on the Inter-Services title was prised open by the Royal Navy, who won another fine Twickenham game 31-20. The two minor headquarters cup finals saw Old Patesians from Cheltenham embellish their promotion to senior status with a narrow 25-24 victory in the intermediate competition over brave Blaydon, for whom promotion to the elite was also achieved, while Halton & Norton won an all-northern Tetley's Bitter Vase final against Hoylake by 36 points to 20. All those occasions enriched the Twickenham scene, as did the *Daily Mail* Schools Day, which was climaxed by a fine performance by Campion School from Essex, who have become a real force at that level of the game and have assumed the Colston's mantle with panache.

Sadly, foot-and-mouth was so widespread that the County Championship was not contested and Twickenham had to make do with a challenge match, in which a most impressive Yorkshire side was too good for Cornwall. The Under 20s, however, did manage to complete their programme, and another cliffhanger saw Surrey beat North Midlands 20-17.

So, in spite of various negative distractions it was a most enjoyable season in England and one can only hope now that the various people who are responsible for the well-being of the game, whether organising leagues or other important facets of the sport, will finally convert affairs from their present battle-zone conditions into efficiently run coherence with common sense operating. There would appear to be too many people who are on personal ego trips, with the good of the game not being part of their plans. And the clubs – particularly the top ones – would do well to remember that they are not owed a living by sponsors or anyone else and that they should try to survive through their own resources, which means that if they cannot afford the world's best players, they should try to achieve results by employing the best of English, and there are plenty of them to go round.

However, the success of the national team – with 18 originally selected players it was under-represented in the Lions tour party – did show that Clive Woodward and his team are 'on the ball', and the ability to select an efficient side to take on Canada and the United States in cap internationals despite the loss of players to the Australia tour party is a reflection of good domestic talent management and organisation. But was it in the best interests of the game's reputation to rush Martin Johnson into the Six Nations team after a suspension for foul play? One worries that one day he may fall really foul of a referee and it would be most embarrassing if it should happen on a Lions tour. However, the future does look bright and I look forward to the next campaign with optimism.

It may not have been a real County Championship final, but Yorkshire still enjoyed their win in the Twickenham showpiece match against Cornwall.

BEHIND SCOTTISH RUGBY.

SCOTLAND – Looking to the future

BY ALAN LORIMER

It was a season in Scotland when the D-word raised its head once more to ignite a further round of rancorous debate on the matter of professional district sides. The issue this time was the setting up of a third district side and, contentiously, the proposal to base it in the Scottish Borders. The principle of increasing the number of Scotland's district sides to three had already been accepted when the findings of the Lord Mackay report were adopted back in 1999. What remained unresolved was the location of the third district. Scotland Director of Rugby Jim Telfer argued that the Borders was the only region in Scotland in which rugby was the main sport.

The importance of a third district was restated as part of the Scottish Rugby Union's vision of rugby in the professional era – a policy document expounding the idea that Scotland could compete internationally only if the professional player base north of the border was expanded. Scotland has only some 70 full-time professional players – inadequate, in the opinion of national coach Ian McGeechan, to provide the necessary competition for international places. Two districts therefore had to become three, with the promise that when economic conditions were right – or, if you like, when the SRU could afford it – a fourth district would be set up in Caledonia.

The Borders district side is scheduled to be operational in season 2002-03. Meanwhile, for next season Edinburgh Reivers and Glasgow Caledonians will become simply Edinburgh and Glasgow and will adopt the two cities as their respective bases.

Not everyone in Scottish rugby, however, finds the district diet digestible. Cue the Scottish Clubs Association (SCA), a recently formed organisation of Premiership clubs with links to the European body of clubs. Their contention is that the money spent on the district sides would be better put into professionalising the clubs. To that end, they proposed an eight-team professional league that would create a base of some 240 professional players, albeit that many of these would be on part-time contracts.

The SCA has consistently argued that strong clubs are what the public are interested in and not artificial districts, which in the association's view constitute an expensive exercise while achieving little. The truth, as always, lies somewhere down the middle of the two lines of thought. Certainly few would argue with the point that the districts have failed to attract large public interest. Nor could their showing in the Welsh/Scottish League, nor for that matter in Europe, point to tangible success. Worse still, a survey conducted by *The Scotsman* newspaper revealed that the degree of public ignorance of the activities of the super-districts was embarrassingly high.

But there is no doubt that the districts route has helped Scotland make a more rapid transition into the professional game. However compelling the arguments for a club-based professional game, there is little chance that Scottish clubs could compete in the major cross-border competitions. Moreover, while critics from within and outwith Scotland cry foul at the notion of teams funded by a union, there is the enormous advantage for Scotland that the SRU has control over its employees, and in the future that could have enormous implications for preventing the dreaded burn-out.

The other frequent criticism from outwith Scotland is that playing district teams in the likes of the European Cup is inherently unfair when such competitions are for clubs. The counter to this is that while Edinburgh Reivers, for example, are a district side, they draw from no greater catchment area than, say, Leicester or Northampton.

Ah yes, Northampton. Their two defeats by Edinburgh Reivers in the European Cup raised hopes that the east coast super-district side could achieve success. But that elusive place in the quarter-finals was not to be forthcoming – largely because of a poor home result against Biarritz.

In the Welsh/Scottish League the Reivers' away record was abysmal while that at home was near impeccable, all of which underlines the point that whatever merit the Welsh/Scottish League has, the major disadvantage is the fortnightly bus run to the Principality – putting a new spin on Reivers being a well-coached side. Reivers also showed themselves to have less appetite for the mucky stuff, their better performances coming late in the season on the drier grounds. To that end, Reivers have been fortunate in that most of their home games have been at Myreside, undoubtedly the best club pitch in Scotland.

The Edinburgh-based district side had seemingly strengthened their squad in the pre-season months by enticing north of the border a number of exiles. In the event, though, it was the younger home-bred players who proved to be the successes for Reivers, the pick of the youthful crop being Simon Taylor, Marcus Di Rollo, Gordon Ross, Kevin Utterson, Craig Smith and Allan Jacobsen.

Among the experienced players, Steve Scott at hooker had an excellent season, but overall it was the elder statesmen who over the piece failed to produce the winning goods. Reivers were unlucky to lose at the beginning of the season Nathan Hines and Andy Lucking, two talented locks who have a future in the game at the top level. As a consequence a number of amateurs were drafted in, among them the impressive Herioter Andrew Dall, the brother of Reivers flanker Graham Dall.

Andrew Dall and Don Mackinnon support Marcus Di Rollo as Edinburgh Reivers go on the attack against Newport.

Across in the west side of the country, it was a similar tale for Glasgow Caledonians. The Reds, as they are popularly known, achieved a modicum of success in the Welsh/Scottish League, their best home win being against Cardiff, but like their Edinburgh-based counterparts they suffered from 'bus syndrome' and consequently chalked up a lamentable away record.

As for Europe, the Reds never stood much chance of making progress to the later stages after being drawn in the same group as the eventual winners, Leicester. Even so, their collapse when a second place qualifying spot was a possibility was disappointing.

Again it was young players who stood out for the Reds, Barry Irving taking his chance to fill in at stand-off after the despatch of Craig Chalmers. Winger Rory Kerr and centre Andy Henderson were young players who proved that they have what it takes, while among the forwards flanker Donnie Macfadyen was the pick of the young brigade.

It was fair to say that high though the standard of super-district rugby may have been it was the BT Scotland Premiership and the BT Cellnet Cup which grabbed the public and media attention. Heriot's were going for a third successive Premiership title, but their aspirations were soon blown apart by some inconsistent form and by the unfaltering mechanism of Hawick's 'Green Machine'. It was an amazing season for the Greens, who turned the clock back two decades to the era when Hawick was synonymous with success in Scottish rugby.

Under the coaching of the irascible Ian Barnes, who never missed an opportunity to have a verbal sideswipe at the SRU, Hawick just got better and better, finishing undefeated and runaway title winners. Barnes had ensured forward supremacy by bringing in two New Zealand props to strengthen his squad. In addition he already had a Scottish Kiwi in flanker Barry Keown, a player who made a massive contribution to Hawick's championship win.

Neil Stenhouse was an inspirational figure in the Hawick side throughout the season.

But there was much more to the Hawick pack than a New Zealand presence. Flanker Roddy Deans was outstanding as a genuine No. 7, Scott McLeod emerged as a real talent at lock, and hooker Matt Landels, if at times unwisely impetuous, nevertheless showed the advantage of having a weighty citizen in the middle of the front row.

The undoubted star of Hawick's season, though, was stand-off Neil Stenhouse, whose range of talents, from prodigious goal-kicking to being able to break defences with a fearsome sidestep, made him hot property.

Hawick also benefited from the steadying influence of their captain and scrum half, Kevin Reid, a player whose talents have so often been understated in the past, and the brilliance of their young centre Stephen Cranston, whose father, Alastair, was a former Scotland midfield player.

As one by one the opposition fell off the leader board, only Melrose hung on, but even the men from the Greenyards could not live with the hot pace that Hawick had set. Melrose, having recovered from an October crisis, produced an impressive string of performances in the second half of the season but much too late to put a brake on Hawick's romp to the line.

At the other end of the first division, it was a disastrous season for Watsonians, who went through their Premiership

campaign without a victory and as a result were relegated with still a third of the championship remaining. Watsonians' record had a distorting effect on the battle to avoid the other relegation place, which, after a tight finish, fell to Jed-Forest.

As Watsonians and Jed slipped through the trap door, Stirling County and Aberdeen Grammar School FP moved in the opposite direction to claim membership of the top tier and in the process provide an almost perfect geographical spread for the first division. Stirling, who undoubtedly have the best rugby nursery in Scotland, used their own produce to reassert themselves, winning the Division Two title with a late charge ahead of Division One newcomers Aberdeen.

Scotland's other major club competition, the BT Cellnet Cup, was in its sixth year, but as yet no side had won the trophy twice. Enter Boroughmuir, defending champions and back in Division One after a slight blip in their distinguished history. The Meggetland men, who had challenged for the Premiership title before falling away, recognised that their destiny lay in the cup.

Their route to the final was straightforward save for a tough semi-final against Heriot's. Against them were the 1997 cup winners, Melrose, who had reached the final by defeating Hawick in a 23-22 thriller at the Greenyards, a match that attracted a crowd that the super-districts could only dream of.

But at Murrayfield it was a one-way contest in the final as Boroughmuir, inspired by their New Zealand-born stand-off Calvin Howarth, retained the cup by producing a brand of fast-paced rugby that left Melrose flagging.

Apart from Howarth it was a day to remember for Scotland wing Derek Stark, making his final appearance on the club stage before retiring from the game. Incredibly Stark was making his fourth appearance in the final, having featured in Boroughmuir's win 12 months earlier, Glasgow Hawks' 1998 victory and the Melrose triumph a year before that.

Club rugby will be poorer without Stark, a much better player than his reviews suggested, and in an era when Scottish rugby, at international level, seems desperately short of pace, Stark had the ability to apply the afterburners when required – a great player to watch in club rugby and one who will be missed.

Boroughmuir captain Tom Penman raises the cup with Derek Stark after his team had overpowered Melrose in the BT Cellnet Cup final.

WALES – An international flavour

BY DAVID STEWART

The links between Welsh rugby and its South African counterpart are long established and continue to prosper, even if the traffic is now rather one way. Who could have predicted that the successful Natal Currie Cup team of the 1990s would play such a prominent role in developing Welsh club football at the start of the next decade? When Ian McIntosh took a Natal squad to Loftus Versfeld in October 1990 to win that province's first national championship for many a long day, their ranks included a New Zealand wing forward called John Plumtree. Shortly afterwards he would be followed into that back row by a tall Zimbabwean called Gary Teichmann. No doubt a teenaged Joost van der Westhuizen was sitting in the stands that day watching the Blue Bulls – in whose colours he would appear for so many years – going down to defeat.

In the 2000-01 season Plumtree coached Swansea to victory in the Welsh/Scottish League, and Teichmann led Newport to victory in the Principality Cup, the club's first trophy of any description for more than 20 years. Teichmann has returned to Durban but not before being anointed with heroic status by the followers of his adoptive club. No sooner had he gone than his old mentor announced he would be making the opposite journey from the Indian Ocean coast to take up a position as director of coaching at Newport, working alongside Allan Lewis. Just for good measure, McIntosh will have the services of the scrum half to whom he gave the first of what turned out to be a record number of Springbok caps. Although the full extent of the scrum half's availability throughout the season is a little unclear, the signing of van der Weisthuizen – one of the true stars of the world game – is a tremendous coup for Tony Brown, the energetic and passionate owner of the Newport club.

While few would dispute the league winners were the best all-round side of the season, the 'story' really was the Black and Ambers. Their line-up may have been a little too 'international' for the taste of traditionalists, but the sense of vitality in and around the club and town was in such stark contrast to the moribund years gone by that only the most soulless of observers could not have shared just a tad of their pleasure at eventual success. In a team which included Matt Pini (Australia/Italy), Matt Mostyn (Ireland but Australian), Andy Marinos (South African), Shane Howarth (New Zealand/Wales), Rod Snow (Canada), Adrian Garvey (Zimbabwe/South Africa), Simon Raiwalui (Fiji but a New Zealander), Peter Buxton (English), it was sometimes a case of spot the local fellow. However, the leadership, organisation and commitment in its broadest sense of their captain were crucial. An early indication of the catalyst for success he would become was the curious habit – at that stage to Welsh eyes – of warming down from 80 minutes' hard rugby by playing a game of tennis, when many of his team-mates had headed for the bar.

Gary Teichmann – hero status, and post-match tennis, at Rodney Parade.

Truth be told, Newport's victories over Ebbw Vale in the semi-finals and Neath in the final were slightly laboured efforts based upon the dominance of their large and experienced pack, with their back-line contributions being efficient rather than inspired. That lack of penetration and ability to 'put a match away' was shown during what many considered to be the best club match of the season in Wales, when before a full house in mid-January in the Heineken Cup the visitors from Munster were permitted to turn a 24-9 deficit at half-time into a 39-24 victory. While disappointed with a result that saw their exclusion from the premier European competition, Mr Brown and his executive staff will have been delighted with the potential shown that night for the future financial welfare of the club as the genuine rugby followers of both teams mingled happily before and after the game in the family-friendly environment at Rodney Parade. But local fans will look to the two newcomers from South Africa to spearhead the club's 2002 Heineken campaign, for which they have qualified by finishing joint third with Llanelli in the league.

Last year we predicted that Swansea would be in the silverware next time around, and with a strong mobile pack and pacy backs they were virtually runaway winners of the Welsh/Scottish League. Plumtree was assisted by former Wales rugby league coach Clive Griffiths. With the thrust of Scott Gibbs and Mark Taylor in the centre complementing the footballing skills of Arwel Thomas and Kevin Morgan behind a pack containing Lions Darren Morris and Colin Charvis, they had plenty of talented material with which to work. Key wins included the double over their nearest and greatest rivals, Llanelli – 28-21 at home in September and 22-23 away just before Christmas – and the home victory over Cardiff before a full house on a gorgeous sunny early November Saturday.

The All Whites' Darren Morris tries to outpace Joe Beardshaw as Swansea play Wasps in the Heineken Cup .

Domestic victories are all very well, but the coach knows more than most that these days it is upon the European stage that his charges are ultimately judged. The New Zealander has made clear his ambition of obtaining a Super-12 post, and the coming season is likely to be his last. Accordingly he will want to banish the memory of that late-January Sunday at Welford Road when Leicester tore apart the All Whites with a performance so comprehensive and clinical that those witnessing it would not only have concluded the Tigers were a good bet to win the competition but also that Swansea had to find another gear if they were to compete effectively at this level. That is the challenge for Plumtree and the squad. There is cause for optimism with new investors in place, the young Wales 'A' out-half Gavin Henson (tipped as the coming man of Welsh rugby) signed to a new contract, and double league and union international Paul Moriaty appointed as defence coach and thus joining big brother Richard on the executive where he serves as team manager.

On the same dark weekend for Welsh club rugby that Swansea exited the quarter-finals of the Heineken Cap, so did Cardiff in another lacklustre performance, this time at Gloucester. For the Blue and Black fans it was like watching an uncanny repeat of their defeat at Llanelli at the same stage of the competition 12 months earlier. Cardiff won the competition in its first year, albeit before the English clubs entered. The ambition of their chairman, Peter Thomas, to see that achievement repeated is well known. Sadly that desire was not compatible with the retention of coach Lynn Howells. One of the decent men of Welsh rugby declined to put his name forward for the newly created director of coaching post, which resulted in the previously unfamiliar Rudy Joubert being recruited following a successful term at the helm of the Boland province in South Africa. In terms of results his objective will be to improve upon the previous season, which saw a second place finish in the league and quarter-final exits in both cups, the defeat in the domestic competition being at St Helens to Swansea in a pulsating match where the result was in doubt right into injury time. The fact that it fell on the weekend between two Six Nations games did not please Graham Henry, and striking a balance that allows players to peak for both club and international commitments is only one of the tasks that Joubert will face.

Perhaps the greatest of these tasks will be unlocking the punishing inconsistency of his team. The high points of their season were impressive home and away wins against Saracens in the Heineken group stage when they out-muscled and out-thought the Watford-based team. The inability to otherwise reproduce such form away from home cost them defeat in Ulster, Toulouse and abjectly in front of the Shed at Gloucester. There is a lingering suspicion that the chemistry of the Cardiff squad is just not quite right. Aside of the outstanding Robert Howley, the most consistent contributions came from experienced South African centre Pieter Muller, before injury brought his season to a premature end, and Canadian wing forward Dan Baugh, whose robust tackling and driving play should render the uglier side of his game unnecessary. The chairman is known to favour developing local young players through the ranks along the lines of the retiring Mike Rayer and the ever-committed Jon Humphreys. The good news is that two outstanding young talents in the threequarter line fulfil that criterion. Jamie Robinson and Craig Morgan both travelled with the Welsh squad to Japan and are strong prospects for the 2003 World Cup. Of greater concern is the mix elsewhere; for example, four former Llanelli forwards, all capped, yet none good enough to be a current international. To compound Joubert's difficulties he has Neil Jenkins, David Young and Martyn Williams returning from less than wonderful Lions tours. However, if he can get it right, Cardiff could again be one of the dominant teams, along with Swansea.

Thomas Castaignède tries to hang on to the rampaging Dan Baugh in Cardiff's Heineken Cup match against Saracens at Vicarage Road.

Llanelli and Bridgend would have something to say about that, since both finished in the top five of the league and thus qualified for places in the Heineken Cup, albeit the Scarlets required a strong late run. The lowest point of their season, and indeed for many a year, was the 16-65 trouncing they received from Cardiff in the Principality Cup at the end of February. For the All Blacks to do that a few years ago was one thing, for their rivals from the capital city to do it was quite another, and for a few rocky days thereafter it looked as if the admirable resilience of their coach Gareth Jenkins might even give way. That ignominy against Cardiff followed an irrational European campaign. An early-season defeat to the aforementioned Gloucester at home was on the verge of being reversed in the return fixture at the end of January, when in injury time, scrum half Elton Moncrieff attempted a desperate drop kick right in front of the Llanelli posts. It was sailing safely under the bar – until it struck a Scarlet shoulder and popped over! With the team only in the league mid-table at this stage, it looked as if the 100 per cent participation of Gareth Jenkins and his assistant Nigel Davies in the Heineken was at an end, but spearheaded by the outstanding Scott Quinnell and his vice-captain, out-half Stephen Jones, a solid finish to the season sees them take their place once again. Whether their squad is strong enough to be truly competitive remains to be seen. With injury keeping both of the Easterby brothers out for long periods last term, Rupert Moon played more than perhaps he anticipated but intends leaving the game to take up the whistle on a full-time basis. Do not bet against him being fast-tracked to top level. A more telling loss is likely to be Dafydd James, who had an outstanding season for the club at outside centre, even though all of his international rugby has thus far been on the wing.

Whether James takes to the Brewery Field any nightmares about Joe Roff remains to be seen, but the chequebook of chairman Leighton Samuel has injected new life and new players, the other internationals being Gareth Thomas from Cardiff and the Ebbw Vale forwards Nathan Budgett and Deinoil Jones. Under the shrewd direction of Dennis John, assisted by the experience and knowledge of former Lions Richard Webster and John Devereux, Bridgend have made steady progress. Whether they quite have the firepower up front to challenge for honours in the year ahead only time will tell. They will be a challenge, particularly at home, for all but the very best. In a sense, their transition has been mirrored by Neath, although the turnaround in the fortunes of this famous club has been even more dramatic. If coach Lynn Jones has not already been granted the freedom of the borough, such an honour cannot be far away. A swift and graceful wing forward during his playing days at the club, Jones, with the assistance of former Welsh captain Gareth Llewellyn at the helm, accomplished the outstanding achievement of piloting a young squad all the way to the cup final. Their semi-final defeat of Swansea was the outstanding 'against the odds' club performance of the season. The wise head of Rowland Phillips, another who trod the path of Welsh international to rugby league and back to union again, will no longer be available, but quality reinforcements are expected in the form of the universally admired Allan Bateman, Barry Williams and out-half Lee Jarvis. With a threequarter line containing crowd favourite Shane Williams, big Tongan David Tiueti, and James Storey (son of athletics commentator Stuart), there will not be a shortage of excitement at the Gnoll in the months ahead.

It can only be good for the club game, and arguably for the international side, to have the likes of Bridgend and Neath becoming genuinely competitive with the four traditional big boys. One hopes their progress will not be at the expense of Pontypridd, whose decline has been feared in this column for a couple of years now. The haemorrhage of top-class players from Sardis Road in recent seasons has finally caught up with the club, and an outstanding team spirit proved insufficient to maintain their own 100 per cent appearance record in the Heineken Cup. However, with talent like centre Sonny Parker and back-row Michael Owen still to hand and a promising bunch of other young players, coach Ritchie Collins does have material to work with. Whether Mike Ruddock will feel quite the same way remains to be seen. His first season of repatriation from Leinster was not a happy one, with Ebbw Vale at the wrong end of the table. Caerphilly battled hard with their enterprising young coaches Gareth Nicholas and Simon King, but it was all too much, as anticipated, for Cross Keys.

So now we move into the seventh season of professional rugby union. There is still further change with the introduction of the Celtic League. At first glance this appears to be something of a hybrid, since the Irish teams will not be playing home and away, unlike those to the north – in other words, the Welsh/Scottish League continues alongside the new competition! It is to be hoped this is a temporary situation only, and it will lead to a levelling-up of playing standards and a greater regularity of home fixtures for clubs. Not the least of their difficulties in coming to terms with the new era of the game has been presenting fans with a reasonably frequent diet of quality matches, thus building up what the marketing men call 'customer loyalty' and promoting cash flow. It has been a difficult road since Vernon Pugh declared the game 'open' in August 1995, but the signs are that standards of fitness, professionalism and quality of performance are improving. For his contribution to that, the club game in Wales owes a warm thank you to the man with a German name, born in a country then called Rhodesia. As he permits his weary body retirement from the rigours of rugby and turns his perceptive mind to matters of business on the east coast of South Africa, we can be sure that each Saturday night he will be checking to see how his former coach is getting on in the southeast corner of Wales, happy in the knowledge that Newport and their supporters will not have forgotten him.

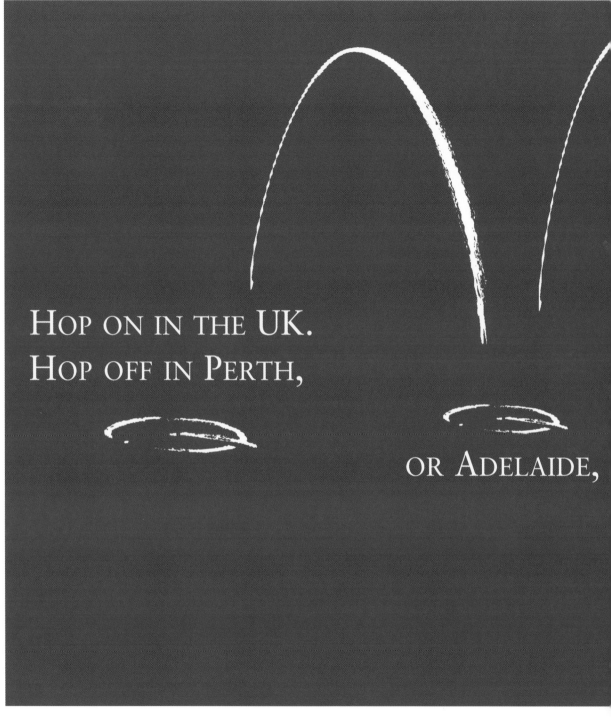

HOP ON IN THE UK.
HOP OFF IN PERTH,

OR ADELAIDE,

Leap on a Cathay Pacific flight to Hong Kong and hop on to any one of our six Australian destinations. We fly three times a day from the UK – and there are 34 flights a week from Hong Kong to Australia, so you can travel when it best suits you. And o

OR CAIRNS,

OR BRISBANE,

OR SYDNEY,

OR MELBOURNE.

...ourse, you fly in style, pampered by the legendary Cathay Pacific service. For further ...etails, contact any IATA travel agent or call us on 020 7747 8888. Because when it ...omes to a choice of Australian destinations, we've got the jump on our competition.

Fly Cathay Pacific. The Heart of Asia.

IRELAND – Dungannon inspired

BY SEAN DIFFLEY

Ken Maginnis, the recently retired MP, was the president of Dungannon last season, and in the second half of the All-Ireland League final at Lansdowne Road he left the committee box and his fellow 'alickadoos' and took a place on the sideline instead. And it was not just excitement, it was much more a gesture of solidarity with his team, who were virtually walking away with the Irish club title and in the process exhibiting the best standard of football ever seen in an All-Ireland final.

In that remarkable second half Dungannon piled on 30 points to a mere three for the pre-match favourites, Cork Constitution. It was not only the surprise of the entire competition but the quality of Dungannon's football was the eye-opener of the season. In the end they demolished Cork Constitution by 46-12.

The Cork side, with Ronan O'Gara at the helm, had dominated the competition all through the season and topped the table when the league part of the All-Ireland finished. But when it came to the final, O'Gara was barred from his club activities because of the demands of the Lions.

The format of the competition has the top four qualified for the semi-finals. It is a situation that some do not approve of, and certainly Cork Constitution have every reason to feel sore after leading the field until that final hurdle. In the semi-finals Dungannon beat Galwegians, and the Cork side beat Young Munster. The IRFU have persevered with this top-four idea and it certainly has yielded dividends in money terms and does end the club season with a decided flourish.

The man who was credited with most of the praise after Dungannon won was their charismatic coach, former Irish lock Willie Anderson. And then there was David Humphreys, a class act if ever there was one. Obviously, Anderson and his playmaker, Humphreys, had burnt the candle at both ends as they devised some of the most thrilling and entertaining back moves seen in Irish rugby for years. Humphreys's personal contribution to Dungannon's total of 46 points was 26 points from five penalty goals, a dropped goal and four conversions.

On his good days David Humphreys reminds us that he is one of the best out-halves in British and Irish rugby. When the Lions selections were announced, Willie Anderson said he was disappointed that Humphreys was not chosen. And in Irish circles there are many who feel that something should be done to accommodate both Humphreys and O'Gara.

Scrum half Stephen Bell got the first of Dungannon's four tries. The others came from Jonathan Bell, Andy Boyd, and a spectacular late one from the dashing Tyrone Howe. Later of course, Howe, one of the most improved wings in the game, got a Lions call-up. Cork Constitution's scores came from three penalty goals by scrum half Brian O'Meara and a dropped goal by Conor Mahony, the out-half who came in for the unenviable job of substituting for the absent Ronan O'Gara.

Willie Anderson – no less than Ken Maginnis – was ecstatic after the All-Ireland triumph. Not since Ulster's win in the European Cup had there been much to celebrate in the North. Dungannon were the first Ulster club to win the All-Ireland, following in the footsteps of St Mary's College, the Leinster side that had won the previous year.

Anderson said: 'We came from behind to win their place in the league proper and then on to win the trophy itself. Dungannon, Tyrone and Ulster can be proud of these guys.'

Up to that point, the club scene and the All-Ireland had been dominated to a remarkable degree by Munster clubs. Cork Constitution were, in fact, the very first winners a decade ago. Then there were the four wins by Shannon. But in recent times the emphasis in Munster has tended to concentrate on the provincial side and their impressive runs in the Heineken European Cup – finalists in 1999-2000 and last year semi-finalists.

The club scene in Ireland is somewhat different to those in England and Wales. Dublin, for instance, a city of just around a million in population, has no fewer than 17 senior clubs in the three divisions of the All-Ireland League. There is a tendency towards amalgamation, but it is very slow. But the big difference is that the players contracted to the four provinces and to the national squad don't often turn out for their clubs.

Willie Anderson (above) and his champion Dungannon team.

Even though he is such an important cog for both Munster and Ireland, Ronan O'Gara did contribute more than his fair share to Cork Constitution until he was no longer available because of Lions selection. In contrast, Brian O'Driscoll, for various

Brian O'Driscoll on one of his few appearances for Blackrock College.

reasons – the calls of Leinster and Ireland – made only the occasional appearance for his club, Blackrock College.

In all, during the competitive season six clubs scored more than 400 points. They were Cork Constitution, Dungannon, University College Cork, Old Belvedere, Bective Rangers and Barnhall. Thomond lost only one match in Division Three but still only finished a point ahead of Barnhall, who amassed 11 bonus points.

If Dungannon were the club of the year, Munster were the province of the year. They were badly served by the foot-and-mouth outbreak and the stringent precautions that had to be taken in a country where agriculture is such a large proportion of the economy. Still, they showed a lot of their old resolve and could well have beaten Stade Français in France in the European Cup semi-finals, even if they were not playing their best. A try was not given by a touch judge when the TV pictures showed it was a clear score. At that stage of the semi-final, a score could have made a big difference. Still, in all the circumstances, Munster had every reason to be proud of their contribution, and not just that of their players but also of their enthusiastic supporters whose behaviour was exemplary.

The foot-and-mouth outbreak, even if the effects were not severe in Ireland, brought about huge disruption to sport in general. With a large proportion of the economy related to agriculture, it was understandable that both north and south of the border stringent regulations were enforced.

The calling-off of the Ireland v England match and its relegation to the following autumn was the most notable rugby casualty, but the ordinary club programme also suffered. The All-Ireland club fixtures were postponed and rural clubs suffered most, naturally. There is the story of the Arklow club in County Wicklow refusing to play a Leinster Provincial Cup game against Boyne, which was near an outbreak some miles to the north. Arklow protested that many of its players were farmers and they couldn't take any risks. But there was a row when the Leinster Branch told them to play or else. They withdrew, very angrily.

The effect of the curtailment of rugby in Ireland meant that Munster were without match practice and paid the penalty. Then there were the problems for the players with aspirations for Lions places who were not at their best at the vital times. The Munster v Rest of Ireland game at Thomond Park, watched by Graham Henry, Andy Robinson and Donal Lenihan when the gates were open again, certainly did no good for some of the Irish contenders, such as Denis Hickie. But by May things were back to normal, and Dungannon, for one, indicated that the enforced rest had done them no harm at all.

Anthony Foley drives forward as Munster take on the Rest of Ireland.

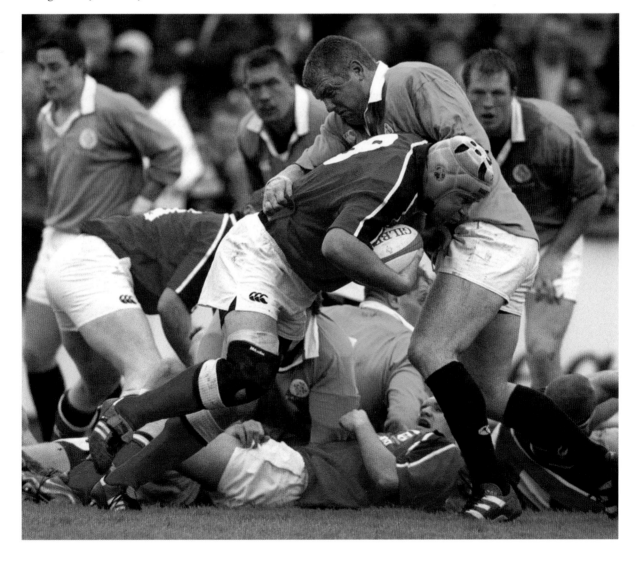

FRANCE – Widening the gap

BY **CHRIS THAU**

It was business as usual for Stade Toulousain in the final of the premier French domestic rugby competition. *Le Rouge et Noir*, displaying the confidence and sure touch of champions in the making, won the French Championship final Mk 100 with remarkable ease. Montferrand tried their best, but that was not good enough against an inspired side, seemingly capable of walking on water. This was Toulouse's sixteenth Bouclier de Brennus from 21 appearances in the final of the oldest club competition in the world.

The secret of this unusual level of consistency at the very top is loyalty, a theme that has underpinned the life and career of the club's chief coach, Guy Novès, a regular with the club since the early 1980s. Novès was himself a valuable member of the championship-winning teams of 1985 and 1986, which were coached by Jean-Claude Skrela and Pierre Villepreux. And in June 2001, when Toulouse won their seventh title under his guidance, Novès became the most successful French club coach ever, having broken the seemingly unbeatable record of Raoul Barrière – the coach of the great Béziers of the 1970s – of six championships from eight attempts.

'Records apart, winning in rugby is about people. And this is where our force is coming from. It is about developing talent, and about nurturing it; it is about an ability to express it; it is about youth and exuberance, about the pleasure of playing and winning. All these have been the values of Toulouse since time immemorial,' Novès said.

Toulouse, deprived of the services of two of their most influential individuals, Emile Ntamack and Isitolo Maka, surprised Montferrand with the vivacity of the challenge. The symbols of Toulouse's everlasting desire for success and perfection were three young men – remember these names – who played a significant role in the clinical demolition of Montferrand: Nicolas Jeanjean, who has since entered history as the youngest full back to have donned the French jersey in an international, scrum half Frédéric Michalak and centre Clément Poitrenaud.

The influential Isitolo Maka gets the ball away against Saracens, but he was not available for Toulouse in their French Championship final against Montferrand.

The following verdict and explanation comes from one of France's most qualified experts, former Béziers regular and coach, Olivier Saisset, currently coaching Perpignan: 'One always felt that Toulouse had more ammunition than Montferrand, although they played their hearts out. Anything Montferrand tried, Toulouse could do better and faster, and they always had something up their sleeve. Montferrand made mistakes under pressure; Toulouse did not. That's what professional rugby is all about.'

Championship number 108 marked the end of an era. The French first division has shrunk to 16 clubs. As a consequence, some of the powers of yesteryear, with former European champions Brive the most notable case, are playing in the 16-strong second division. But while the budgets of Brive, Grenoble and Toulon – which at £2.6, £2, and £1.8 million respectively are comparable to those of some of the premier division clubs – suggest an early return to the ranks of the elite, the fate of their former first division fellow travellers Auch, Périgueux, Aurillac and Montpellier is likely to be determined by their comparatively limited resources of £0.8, £1.2, £1.4, and £1.4 million respectively.

Another by-product of the restructuring of French rugby is the emerging political alliance between the players' trade union chaired by former international prop Serge Simon and the Professional League led by Serge Blanco. One of the more controversial ideas to have emerged from a meeting in May between French Sports Minister Marie-Georges Buffet, FFR President Bernard Lapasset and Blanco was the proposal to hold the matches of the Six Nations on consecutive weekends.

Celebrations – Toulouse-style.

ITALY – Revenge of the Romans

BY **CHRIS THAU**

Will Diego Dominguez have another go, or won't he? The fact that the possible return to international action of the diminutive Italo-Argentine still dominates the pages of the Italian media is indicative of the degree of dissatisfaction in the aftermath of Italy's second unsuccessful Six Nations campaign and the moderately productive summer tour to Namibia, South Africa, Uruguay and Argentina. Leaving aside the soccer mentality of the Italian journalists, the Dominguez debate underlines the problems of Italy, battling to reconcile the demands of professionalism with a feeble domestic structure and a tempestuous desire for success. After two years and ten matches, Italy's Six Nations card read: played ten, won one, lost nine; while the 2001 world tour ended with negative equity as well: played seven, won three, lost four.

Unfortunately, the bare figures reflect neither the improvement in quality and mentality of the new-look Italy nor that in the quality of their play – displayed in patches admittedly – against top international opposition. There is no mention of the successful recruitment policy of Brad Johnstone, the charismatic New Zealander, whose contract as national coach of Italy is currently under review. The promotion of a crop of young players of talent and ambition to the national squad and the development of strength in depth in Italian rugby at its elite end do not appear in the statistics and remain a closely guarded secret to all but a few media men and administrators.

The win against Scotland in the opening match of Italy's first Six Nations campaign has fuelled unrealistic expectations among media, supporters and administrators. The reality of the world's oldest international competition is different and has been keenly felt by all concerned. During his days as national coach, Georges Coste had recruited, trained and fine-tuned a commando unit of about a dozen or so players of talent and commitment to be able to hold their own against any opposition within any context. However, as soon as injury, loss of form, or 'political' reasons depleted this hard core of trusted warriors, Italy became vulnerable. Moreover, the 'soldiers' themselves started to believe in their own rhetoric and openly challenged the methods and the man who brought them success and recognition.

Italy peaked in terms of performance and quality of outcome during the 1994 Australian tour and had an impressive RWC campaign in 1995, when lack of concentration and a bit of bad luck prevented a deserved quarter-final berth. The professional era hit Italian 'shamateur' rugby with a vengeance. Some clubs, including the once-famous Mediolanum Milan, dropped out of the elite or folded altogether. Coste's high standards failed to be replicated elsewhere in Italy and he had found himself battling to do two jobs, as coach of the national team and technical director of the Federation.

Georges Coste was largely responsible for the rise of Italian rugby in the mid-1990s but could not be persuaded to return as national coach in place of Brad Johnstone.

However, his diet of rigour, application and concentration brought Italy within inches of glory in 1998, in an RWC 99 qualifier in Huddersfield, when a refereeing error deprived Giovanelli and his team of a famous and deserved win against England. However, Coste's uncompromising methods, his relentless drive for perfection and his no-nonsense approach brought him into conflict with the players. Player power in Italian rugby manifested itself for the first time during the ill-fated summer tour to South Africa in 1995, when the players rebelled against the Frenchman. A combination of factors, from resentment at his methods to the parlous state of their financial deals as

Diego Dominguez bids farewell to international rugby after Italy's game against France - will he return?

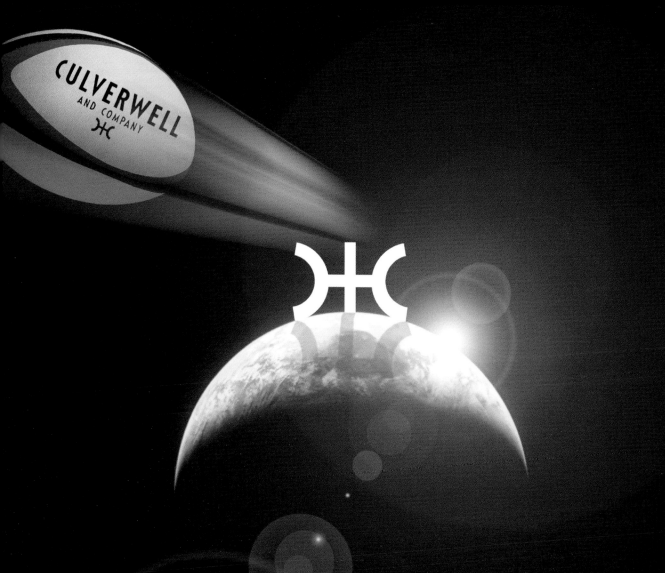

professionals and the poor results on tour, as well as a heavy seasoning of Machiavellian machinations, led to the uprising.

Coste, a benign dictator who believed in consensus, stepped down – although fully supported by the Italian Federation President Giancarlo Dondi – leaving his assistant, Massimo Mascioletti, in charge. The rest is history, with Italy tumbling from disaster to disaster, including the final indignity of losing to Tonga in injury time in RWC 99. After the World Cup, Mascioletti was sent to coach the youth team, with new man Brad Johnstone appointed in the aftermath of his successful two-year stint with Fiji.

While the win against Scotland in the Six Nations brought about a state of euphoria, the value of Johnstone's stock went down with every subsequent defeat, irrespective of the way the team played and the circumstances. The public voted with their feet, too, and after a couple of full houses during the first season, the stands of the National Stadium held more visiting fans than Italian supporters during the second year. Unfortunately, a state of collective amnesia prevented Italian pundits from recalling the simple fact that it took France nearly ten years before they became competitive against the British and Irish in the then Five Nations – it may take Italy even longer in the new professional environment.

Former Italian captain Massimo Giovanelli is exploring the possibility that an eye operation may enable him to play again.

In addition, the inevitable conflict with the players, torn between professional contracts with the clubs and the demands of the national team, materialised as expected. Johnstone, a disciplinarian, was compelled to eat humble pie after being forced to abandon his publicised decision to suspend Alessandro Troncon. After that, the names of his possible successors started to be traded freely in the Italian newspapers.

However, the burly New Zealander and his assistant, Samoan utility back Matthew Vaea, appear more resilient than originally thought. While many of those contacted by the Federation, including the coach of Benetton Treviso, Alain Texidor, have been reluctant to accept the poisoned chalice, a new idea put forward at the FIR executive in July seems to be gathering support – that two or three former players of standing are recruited by the CEO, Fabrizio Gaetaniello, to assist Johnstone with the national team.

Georges Coste also turned down the approach to return as Italian national coach, while his predecessor, Bertrand 'Mitou' Fourcarde, has accepted the position of technical director, a much-needed development which will free the national coach to concentrate solely on the national team. The plan to groom Massimo Giovanelli as national team manager ended in failure, and the former Italian captain, while trying to finish his degree in architecture, is seeking medical opinion in Switzerland about the suitability of an eye operation, which may revive his playing career.

The stock of Frenchman Alain Texidor skyrocketed on the Italian market after he coached his club, Benetton Treviso, to a comfortable 33-13 win over Craig Green's Calvisano in the final of the Italian Championship, but Rome's Gilbert Doucet and Dawie Snyman, offered a contract with the ambitious Parma, may well end up in some advisory role within the new coaching set-up.

So, will Dominguez grace the international scene again this season? Informed sources suggest that the Stade Français fly half will be tempted out of retirement for the last time by a very substantial offer from the Italian Federation, which will maintain his status as the highest-paid outside half in international rugby. That may increase Italy's chances of increasing their winning rate in the championship, so far confined to their singular success against Scotland in February 2000.

A SUMMARY OF THE SEASON 2000-01

BY **BILL MITCHELL**

INTERNATIONAL RUGBY

AUSTRALIA TO JAPAN & EUROPE
OCTOBER & NOVEMBER 2000

Opponents	Results
Japan President's XV	W 64-13
FRANCE	W 18-13
SCOTLAND	W 30-9
ENGLAND	L 18-21

Played 4 Won 3 Lost 1

NEW ZEALAND TO EUROPE
NOVEMBER 2000

Opponents	Results
FRANCE	W 39-26
FRANCE	L 33-42
ITALY	W 56-19

Played 3 Won 2 Lost 1

USA TO SCOTLAND & WALES
NOVEMBER 2000

Opponents	Results
SCOTLAND	L 6-53
Scotland Development XV	L 17-49
Cross Keys	W 22-7
Wales Development XV	L 20-46
WALES	L 11-42

Played 5 Won 1 Lost 4

SAMOA TO WALES & SCOTLAND
NOVEMBER 2000

Opponents	Results
WALES	L 6-50
Scotland 'A'	L 24-37
SCOTLAND	L 8-31

Played 3 Lost 3

ARGENTINA TO ENGLAND
NOVEMBER 2000

Opponents	Results
Combined Services	W 44-7
ENGLAND	L 0-19

Played 2 Won 1 Lost 1

SA TO ARGENTINA & BRITISH ISLES
NOVEMBER & DECEMBER 2000

Opponents	Results
Argentina 'A'	W 32-21
ARGENTINA	W 37-33
Ireland 'A'	L 11-28
IRELAND	W 28-18
Wales 'A'	W 34-15
WALES	W 23-13
English National Divisions	L 30-35
ENGLAND	L 17-25
Barbarians	W 41-31

Played 9 Won 6 Lost 3

ENGLAND TO NORTH AMERICA
JUNE 2001

Opponents	Results
CANADA	W 22-10
British Columbia	W 41-19
CANADA	W 59-20
United States 'A'	W 83-21
UNITED STATES	W 48-19

Played 5 Won 5

WALES TO JAPAN
JUNE 2001

Opponents	Results
Suntory	L 41-45
Japan XV	W 33-22
JAPAN	W 64-10
Pacific Barbarians	L 16-36
JAPAN	W 53-30

Played 5 Won 3 Lost 2

ARGENTINA TO NEW ZEALAND
JUNE 2001

Opponents	Results
Counties	W 70-26
Thames Valley	W 26-12
NEW ZEALAND	L 19-67
New Zealand Maori	L 24-43

Played 4 Won 2 Lost 2

FRANCE TO SOUTH AFRICA & NEW ZEALAND JUNE 2001

Opponents	Results
SOUTH AFRICA	W 32-23
SOUTH AFRICA	L 15-20
NEW ZEALAND	L 12-37

Played 3 Won 1 Lost 2

ITALY TO SOUTHERN AFRICA & SOUTH AMERICA JUNE & JULY 2001

Opponents	Results
Namibia President's XV	W 58-16
NAMIBIA	W 49-24
South African Barbarians	L 11-42
SOUTH AFRICA	L 14-60
URUGUAY	W 14-3
Argentina 'A'	L 12-62
ARGENTINA	L 17-38

Played 7 Won 3 Lost 4

BRITISH ISLES TO AUSTRALIA JUNE & JULY 2001

Opponents	Results
Western Australia	W 116-10
Queensland President's XV	W 83-6
Queensland Reds	W 42-8
Australia 'A'	L 25-28
New South Wales Waratahs	W 41-24
New South Wales Country	W 46-3
AUSTRALIA	W 29-13
ACT Brumbies	W 30-28
AUSTRALIA	L 14-35
AUSTRALIA	L 23-29

Played 10 Won 7 Lost 3

LLOYDS TSB SIX NATIONS CHAMPIONSHIP 2001

Results

Italy	22	Ireland	41
Wales	15	England	44
France	16	Scotland	6
England	80	Italy	23
Ireland	22	France	15
Scotland	28	Wales	28
England	43	Scotland	3
Italy	19	France	30
France	35	Wales	43
Scotland	23	Italy	19
England	48	France	19
Italy	23	Wales	33

Wales v Ireland, Ireland v England and Scotland v Ireland all postponed owing to foot-and-mouth outbreak

	P	W	D	L	F	A	Pts
England	4	4	0	0	215	60	8
Wales	4	2	1	1	119	130	5
Ireland	2	2	0	0	63	37	4
France	5	2	0	3	115	138	4
Scotland	4	1	1	2	60	106	3
Italy	5	0	0	5	106	207	0

PAN-AMERICAN CHAMPIONSHIP MAY 2001

(HELD IN UNITED STATES & CANADA)

Results

Canada	19	United States	10
Argentina	32	Uruguay	27
United States	16	Argentina	24
Canada	14	Uruguay	8
Uruguay	31	United States	28
Canada	6	Argentina	20

	P	W	D	L	F	A	Pts
Argentina	3	3	0	0	96	49	9
Canada	3	2	0	1	39	38	7
Uruguay	3	1	0	2	66	74	5
United States	3	0	0	3	54	94	3

PACIFIC RIM TRI-NATIONS CHAMPIONSHIP 2001 (TO DATE)

Results

Samoa	20	Tonga	19
Fiji	27	Samoa	36
Fiji	25	Tonga	20

OTHER INTERNATIONAL & REPRESENTATIVE MATCHES

EUROPEAN NATIONS

Spain	29	Russia	30
Portugal	12	Georgia	36
Russia	23	Georgia	25
Romania	47	Portugal	0
Spain	12	Romania	27

OTHER

Ireland	78	Japan	9
Romania	3	Ireland	37
Italy	17	Canada	22
Wales 'A'	9	New Zealand 'A'	30
Italy	37	Romania	17
Romania	9	New Zealand 'A'	82
Munster	24	Rest of Ireland	22
Australia	41	NZ Maori	29
New Zealand	50	Samoa	6

TOGETHER WE CAN BUILD A BETTER FUTURE

We are proud to support the Wooden Spoon Society

PRICEWATERHOUSECOOPERS 🅿️

SIX NATIONS 'A' CHAMPIONSHIP

Results

Wales	19	England	19
Italy	16	Ireland	68
France	15	Scotland	8
England	44	Italy	3
Ireland	23	France	55
Scotland	42	Wales	20
England	60	Scotland	20
Italy	16	France	37
France	27	Wales	22
Scotland	33	Italy	13
England	23	France	22
Italy	16	Wales	25

Wales v Ireland, Ireland v England and Scotland v Ireland all postponed owing to foot-and mouth outbreak

	P	W	D	L	F	A	Pts
France	5	4	0	1	156	92	8
England	4	3	1	0	146	64	7
Scotland	4	2	0	2	103	108	4
Wales	4	1	1	2	86	104	3
Ireland	2	1	0	1	91	71	2
Italy	5	0	0	5	64	207	0

UNDER 21 INTERNATIONAL RESULTS

SIX NATIONS

Wales	21	England	12
Italy	10	Ireland	61
France	22	Scotland	15
Ireland	13	France	33
Scotland	18	Wales	31
England	47	Italy	18
England	62	Scotland	29
Italy	10	France	42
France	18	Wales	0
Scotland	27	Italy	9
England	10	France	8
Italy	3	Wales	16

Wales v Ireland, Ireland v England and Scotland v Ireland all postponed owing to foot-and-mouth outbreak

	P	W	D	L	F	A	Pts
France	5	4	0	1	123	48	8
England	4	3	0	1	131	76	6
Wales	4	3	0	1	68	51	6
Ireland	2	1	0	1	74	43	2
Scotland	4	1	0	3	89	124	2
Italy	5	0	0	5	50	193	0

OTHER UNDER 21 REPRESENTATIVE MATCH
England U21 'A'　27　Wales U21 'A'　26

JUNIOR WORLD CUP 2001

(HELD IN CHILE)

Semi-finals

Australia	18	New Zealand	35
France	28	Wales	13

Third-place play-off

Australia	43	Wales	24

Final

New Zealand	36	France	23

TESCO 18 GROUP FESTIVAL
APRIL 2001

Results

England	23	Wales	10
Scotland	25	Italy	19
England	13	Scotland	9
Wales	40	Italy	10
Scotland	30	Wales	14
England	59	Italy	5

	P	W	D	L	F	A	Pts
England	3	3	0	0	95	24	6
Scotland	3	2	0	1	64	46	4
Wales	3	1	0	2	64	63	2
Italy	3	0	0	3	34	124	0

OTHER SCHOOLS AND AGE GROUP MATCHES

Results

Scotland U18 'A'	25	England 16 Grp	20
England 18 Grp	18	Wales 18 Grp	3
Wales 16 Grp	15	England 16 Grp	9

WORLD STUDENT CHAMPIONSHIPS
AUGUST 2000

(HELD IN ITALY)

Quarter-finals

England	30	Italy	11
France	52	Russia	13
Scotland	25	Uruguay	24
South Africa	52	Japan	22

Semi-finals

England	15	France	34
Scotland	28	South Africa	38

Third-place play-off

England	18	Scotland	25

Final

France	39	South Africa	24

THE TIMES INTERNATIONAL UNIVERSITIES TROPHY

Final
U P. Sabatie, T'louse 28   Trinity Coll, Dublin 17

OTHER STUDENT & UNIVERSITY INTERNATIONALS 2000-01

Results

Scotland	22	Wales	19
England	33	Scotland	10

HONG KONG SEVENS

Cup Final

New Zealand	34	Fiji	5

Plate Final

United States	31	Wales	26

Bowl Final

Hong Kong	47	West Indies	5

IRB SEVENS SERIES FINALS

Argentina (Mar del Plata) Melrose Cup:

New Zealand	31	Australia	12

New Zealand (Wellington):

Australia	19	Fiji	17

China (Shanghai):

Australia	19	South Africa	12

Malaysia (Kuala Lumpur):

Australia	19	New Zealand	17

Japan (Tokyo):

New Zealand	26	Australia	12

England (Twickenham):

New Zealand	19	Australia	12

Wales (Cardiff & Newport):

New Zealand	31	Australia	5

New Zealand win the IRB World Sevens Series

OTHER INTERNATIONAL SEVENS FINALS

Dubai:

New Zealand	38	Fiji	12

Oceania:

Cook Islands	24	Tonga	21

Uruguay (Punta del Este):

Argentina	26	New Zealand	21

TRI NATIONS (TO DATE)

Results

South Africa	3	New Zealand	12
South Africa	20	Australia	15
New Zealand	15	Australia	23

WOMEN'S SIX NATIONS CHAMPIONSHIP 2000-01

Results

France	13	Scotland	0
Spain	42	Ireland	0
Wales	0	England	18
England	28	Spain	12
Scotland	22	Ireland	0
England	39	Scotland	0
Spain	6	France	0
France	24	Wales	3
Scotland	19	Spain	8

Programme incomplete

OTHER WOMEN'S INTERNATIONAL AND REPRESENTATIVE MATCHES

Results

Scotland 'A'	12	Wales 'A'	26
Scotland Students	14	Wales Dev't	34
Australia	19	England	41
Australia	5	England	15
New Zealand	15	England	10
New Zealand	17	England	22

FIRA WOMEN'S CHAMPIONSHIP

(HELD IN LILLE, FRANCE)

Semi-finals

England	8	Spain	15
France	6	Scotland	9

Third-place play-off

England	32	France	23

Final

Scotland	15	Spain	3

CLUB, COUNTY AND DIVISIONAL RUGBY

ENGLAND

Tetley's Bitter Cup
Quarter-finals

Harlequins	11	Northampton	6
Leicester	41	Saracens	24
Newcastle	33	London Irish	20
Sale	59	Waterloo	12

Semi-finals

Newcastle	37	Sale	25
Harlequins	22	Leicester	18

Final

Newcastle	30	Harlequins	27

Zurich Premiership

	P	W	D	L	F	A	BP	Pts
Leicester	22	18	1	3	571	346	8	82
Wasps	22	16	0	6	663	428	10	74
Bath	22	14	0	8	680	430	14	70
N'hampton	22	13	0	9	518	463	7	59
Saracens	22	12	0	10	589	501	10	58
Newcastle	22	11	0	11	554	568	13	57
Gloucester	22	10	0	12	473	526	8	48
Ldn Irish	22	10	1	11	476	576	3	45
Bristol	22	9	1	12	443	492	6	44
Sale	22	8	1	13	561	622	9	43
Harlequins	22	7	0	15	440	538	10	38
Rotherham	22	2	0	20	335	813	4	12

Relegated: Rotherham

Zurich Premiership Play-offs
Quarter-finals

Leicester	24	London Irish	11
Wasps	18	Gloucester	6
Bath	18	Newcastle	9
Northampton	45	Saracens	17

Semi-finals

Leicester	17	Northampton	13
Wasps	31	Bath	36

Final

Leicester	22	Bath	10

National Leagues
1st Division Champions: Leeds
Runners-up: Worcester
2nd Division Champions: Bracknell
Runners-up: Rugby
3rd Division North Champions: Stourbridge
Runners-up: Sedgley Park
3rd Division South Champions: Plymouth A
Runners-up: Launceston

The programmes for Division 2 and Division 3 North were not completed

Intermediate Cup Final
Old Patesians	25	Blaydon	24

Tetley's Bitter Vase Final (Junior)
Halton & Norton	36	Hoylake	20

Tetley's Bitter County Championship Challenge Match
Yorkshire	47	Cornwall	19

Tetley's Bitter U20 County Championship Final
Surrey	20	North Midlands	17

The senior County Championship was not played owing to the foot-and-mouth outbreak

University Match
Oxford U	19	Cambridge U	16

University Second Teams Match
CU LX Club	16	OU Greyhounds	18

University U21 Match
Oxford U	21	Cambridge U	3

Other University U21 Match
OU Whippets	15	CU U21 'A'	8

Colleges Match
Oxford U	12	Cambridge U	31

Women's University Match
Cambridge U	5	Oxford U	15

Halifax British Universities Sports Assoc'n
Men's Final
Exeter U	24	Northumbria U	24

(Aet: Exeter U won on 3-2 try count)
Women's Final
Loughborough U	12	Oxford U	5

Hospitals Cup Winners: Guy's Hospital
Inter-Services Champions: Royal Navy
National County Sevens Cup Winners: Middlesex
National County Sevens Plate Winners: Hampshire
Eurobet Middlesex Sevens Cup Winners: Penguins
Eurobet Middlesex Sevens Plate Winners: London Irish
The Army Rosslyn Park Schools Sevens Festival Winners: Wellington College
Colts Winners: Wellington College
Junior Winners: Whitgift School
Open Finals: *Cancelled – grounds flooded*
Girls Finals: *Cancelled – grounds flooded*

Daily Mail Schools Day (at Twickenham)
U18 Cup Winners: Campion School
U18 Vase Winners: King Henry VIII School, Coventry
U15 Cup Winners: Eltham College
Women's National Cup Final
Richmond	35	Wasps	26

We've really put our balls on THE line this time!

You can now spread bet on the net!

SportingIndex.com

World Leaders in Sports Spread Betting

FREE £250 BET! FOR ALL NEW CLIENTS TERMS AND CONDITIONS APPLY. SEE SITE FOR DETAILS.

INTERACTIVE · LIVE · ON-LINE

WALES

Principality Cup
Semi-finals

Newport	17	Ebbw Vale	12
Neath	26	Swansea	17

Final

Newport	13	Neath	8

Anglo-Welsh Challenge Match

Cardiff	29	Leicester	17

Welsh/Scottish League Premier Division

	P	W	D	L	F	A	T	Pts
Swansea	22	18	0	4	809	357	102	54
Cardiff	22	16	0	6	665	410	69	48
Llanelli	22	14	0	8	663	484	76	42
Newport	22	14	0	8	660	338	71	42
Bridgend	22	13	0	9	637	479	71	39
Neath	22	12	1	9	639	543	76	37
G'gow Cals	22	12	0	10	645	608	78	36
E'burgh Rs	22	11	0	11	540	667	55	33
Pontypridd	22	10	0	12	635	541	66	30
Caerphilly	22	5	1	15	464	784	50	16
Ebbw Vale	22	5	0	17	428	741	44	15
Cross Keys	22	1	0	21	247	1100	32	3

Champions: Swansea
Relegated: Cross Keys

Welsh National Leagues
Division One

	P	W	D	L	F	A	T	Pts
Aberavon	30	26	1	3	820	358	114	79
Dunvant	30	22	1	7	817	518	102	67
Pontypool	30	20	2	8	762	515	93	62
C'then Qns	30	17	2	11	638	524	68	53
Rumney	30	14	2	14	561	662	65	44
G'gan Wdrs	30	13	1	16	781	799	93	40
Treorchy	30	13	1	16	629	771	63	40
Bonymaen	30	13	1	16	539	620	59	40
Newbridge	30	13	1	16	539	628	50	40
Llamharan	30	13	0	17	654	774	70	39
Blackwood	30	12	2	16	578	565	56	38
Tondu	30	12	1	17	628	566	84	37
Merthyr	30	12	1	17	510	743	47	37
Llandovery	30	12	0	18	687	760	83	36
Abertillery	30	11	2	17	561	674	54	35
Abercynon	30	7	2	21	496	720	60	23

Promoted: Aberavon (Champions)
Relegated: Abertillery, Abercynon

2nd Division Champions: Bedwas
Runners-up: Whitland
3rd Div East Champions: Beddau
Runners-up: Pencoed
3rd Div West Champions: Llangennech
Runners-up: Seven Sisters

SCOTLAND

Inter-District Championship

	P	W	D	L	F	A	B	Pts
Scot Exiles	4	4	0	0	89	58	1	17
Scot B'ders	4	2	0	2	130	96	4	12
Edinburgh	4	2	0	2	94	86	3	11
Glasgow	4	2	0	2	50	100	0	8
Caledonia	4	0	0	4	69	92	1	4

BT Cellnet Cup Final

Boroughmuir	39	Melrose	15

BT Cellnet Shield Final

Edinburgh Ac	43	Haddington	23

BT Cellnet Bowl Final

Lenzie	25	Cartha Qn's Pk	20

Scottish Sevens Winners:
Kelso: West of Scotland
Selkirk: Melrose
Melrose: Barbarians
Peebles: Peebles
Earlston: Jed-Forest
Jed-Forest: Jed-Forest
Gala: Kelso
Kings of Sevens: Jed-Forest

BT Scotland Premiership
Division One

	P	W	D	L	F	A	BP	Pts
Hawick	18	16	2	0	559	244	6	74
Melrose	18	12	1	5	501	288	10	60
B'muir	18	10	2	6	572	365	10	54
Heriot's FP	18	8	1	9	399	377	10	44
Currie	18	8	2	8	350	379	7	43
G'gow Hks	18	8	0	10	355	383	8	40
Gala	18	8	0	10	372	433	7	39
Kirkcaldy	18	8	0	10	412	475	7	39
Jed-Forest	18	8	0	10	323	437	5	37
Watsonians	18	0	0	18	251	712	4	4

Champions: Hawick
Relegated: Jed-Forest, Watsonians

Division Two

	P	W	D	L	F	A	BP	Pts
Stirling C'ty	18	14	2	2	402	259	4	66
A'deen GSFP	18	11	1	6	502	328	13	59
Kelso	18	10	0	8	322	304	4	44
Ayr	18	9	1	8	365	371	4	42
Peebles	18	9	0	9	334	381	4	40
E Kilbride	18	7	1	10	338	349	8	38
Selkirk	18	7	2	9	247	337	4	36
W of Scot'd	18	6	2	10	318	408	7	35
Biggar	18	6	1	11	284	292	7	33
E'burgh Ac	18	6	0	12	297	380	9	33

Promoted: Stirling County (Champions),
Aberdeen GSFP
Relegated: Biggar, Edinburgh Academicals

IRELAND

Inter-Provincial Championship

	P	W	D	L	F	A	Pts
Munster	6	4	1	1	143	107	9
Ulster	6	4	0	2	142	111	8
Leinster	6	2	1	3	109	111	5
Connacht	6	1	0	5	100	175	2

AIB All-Ireland League
Division One

	P	W	D	L	F	A	B	Pts
Cork Const	15	12	0	3	420	265	10	58
Galwegians	15	11	0	4	338	254	7	51
Dungannon	15	10	1	4	435	283	8	50
Y Munster	15	10	0	5	364	241	8	48
Ballymena	15	8	1	6	384	326	10	44
St Mary's C	15	9	1	5	302	276	4	42
Garryowen	15	7	2	6	317	343	4	36
Shannon	15	7	1	7	347	307	5	35
Blackrock C	15	7	1	7	317	302	5	35
Terenure C	15	6	1	8	323	358	4	30
Clontarf	15	6	0	9	343	442	5	29
Lansdowne	15	5	2	8	259	300	4	28
Buccaneers	15	5	0	10	267	334	6	26
De la Salle-								
Palmerston	15	5	0	10	266	382	4	24
Old Cresc	15	4	0	11	306	422	5	21
Belfast H	15	3	0	12	265	418	7	19

Championship final
Cork Constitution 12   Dungannon   46

Division Two

	P	W	D	L	F	A	Pts
UCD	15	12	1	2	419	245	58
Co Carlow	15	12	0	3	377	195	57
Old Belvedere	15	11	1	3	415	266	55
Bective Rangers	15	11	0	4	425	250	54
UL Bohemians	15	7	1	7	330	288	37
Dolphin	15	7	1	7	361	328	34
Ballynahinch	15	5	4	6	268	276	32
Wanderers	15	6	2	7	251	260	32
Midleton	15	6	1	8	223	280	31
Malone	15	6	1	8	246	316	30
City of Derry	15	5	1	9	294	320	29
Sundays Well	15	6	1	8	271	324	29
UCC	15	6	0	9	240	282	28
Portadown	15	6	0	9	227	356	26
Greystones	15	4	1	10	287	365	23
Old Wesley	15	3	0	12	163	446	14

FRANCE

French Championship
Pool One

	P	W	D	L	F	A	Pts
Castres	18	14	0	4	558	324	46
Stade Fr	18	12	2	4	624	409	44
Perpignan	18	11	0	7	492	452	40
Agen	18	10	1	7	480	385	39
Béziers	18	10	0	8	515	414	38
B-Bordeaux	18	8	0	10	402	533	34
Pau	18	8	0	10	427	404	34
M-de-Marsan	18	5	0	13	337	491	28
Périgueux	18	1	0	17	279	776	20

Pool Two

	P	W	D	L	F	A	Pts
Montferrand	20	15	1	4	633	404	51
S T'lousain	20	14	0	6	651	380	48
Biarritz	20	13	1	6	594	408	47
Colomiers	20	11	0	9	474	440	42
Narbonne	20	10	0	10	579	519	40
Dax	20	10	0	10	419	506	40
La Rochelle	20	9	0	11	434	537	38
Grenoble	20	9	0	11	428	479	38
Brive	20	8	0	12	439	563	36
Aurillac	20	7	0	13	464	577	34
Auch	20	3	0	17	329	622	26

Quarter-finals

Castres	37	Colomiers	26
Stade Toulousain	20	Perpignan	15
Stade Français	19	Biarritz	35
Montferrand	33	Agen	21

Semi-finals

Montferrand	16	Biarritz	9
Stade Toulousain	32	Castres	21

Final

Stade Toulousain	34	Montferrand	22

ITALY

Italian Championship
Final

Benetton Treviso	33	Calvisano	13

NEW ZEALAND

First Division Championship 2000
Final

Canterbury	29	Wellington	34

Ranfurly Shield Holders: Canterbury

AUSTRALIA

Champions 2000: ACT Brumbies

SOUTH AFRICA

Currie Cup 2000

Semi-finals

Natal Coastal Sharks	29	Free State Cheetahs	15
Western Stormers	43	Golden Lions	22

Final

Natal C'tal Sharks 15   W Stormers   25

BARBARIANS

Opponents	Results
Germany	W 47-19
SOUTH AFRICA	L 31-41
East Midlands	L 12-62
Border League XV	L 24-31
WALES	W 40-38
SCOTLAND	W 74-31
ENGLAND	W 43-29

Played 7 Won 4 Lost 3

SUPER-12 TOURNAMENT 2001

Final Table

	P	W	D	L	F	A	BP	Pts
Brumbies	11	8	0	3	348	204	8	40
Sharks	11	8	0	3	322	246	6	38
Cats	11	7	0	4	285	244	6	34
Reds	11	6	0	5	326	350	8	32
Highlanders	11	6	0	5	284	295	5	29
Chiefs	11	6	0	5	301	330	4	28
Stormers	11	5	0	6	278	285	6	26
Waratahs	11	5	0	6	306	302	5	25
Hurricanes	11	5	0	6	291	316	5	25
Crusaders	11	4	0	7	307	330	7	23
Blues	11	4	0	7	243	298	4	21
Bulls	11	2	0	9	241	378	3	11

Semi-finals

Brumbies	30	Reds	6
(Canberra)			
Sharks	30	Cats	12
(Durban)			

Final

Brumbies	36	Sharks	6
(Canberra)			

Team names:
ACT Brumbies
Canterbury Crusaders
Otago Highlanders
Golden Cats
Western Stormers
Auckland Blues
Queensland Reds
Wellington Hurricanes
NSW Waratahs
Waikato Chiefs
Northern Bulls
Coastal Sharks

EUROPEAN CUP

Quarter-finals

Stade Français	36	Pau	19
Gloucester	21	Cardiff	15
Leicester	41	Swansea	10
Munster	38	Biarritz	29

Semi-finals

Leicester	19	Gloucester	15
Stade Français	16	Munster	15

Final

Stade Français	30	Leicester	34

EUROPEAN SHIELD

Quarter-finals

Agen	31	Béziers	0
Narbonne	34	Perpignan	24
Brive	13	Harlequins	20
Newcastle	61	Mont-de-Marsan	23

Semi-finals

Agen	15	Narbonne	22
Harlequins	17	Newcastle	12

Final

Harlequins	42	Narbonne	33
(After extra time)			

PREVIEW OF
THE SEASON
2001-02

KEY PLAYERS 2001-02
BY IAN ROBERTSON

ENGLAND

RICHARD HILL

England can boast arguably the best pack in world rugby and they can certainly boast one of the very best back rows. Not only are the three players – Richard Hill, Lawrence Dallaglio and Neil Back – each outstanding as individuals but they have developed into a tremendous combination. If the other two tend to grab the headlines, Richard Hill is every bit as important to England. He is fast enough to play at open-side, which makes him just about the quickest blind-side flanker in international rugby. He is a great support player in attack and one of the most committed and aggressive tacklers in defence.

Hill seems to have been in the side for a long time, but in fact he only won his first cap for England in 1997 against Scotland. In his first year with England he was selected for the Lions tour to South Africa and he played in two of the three Test matches. After another great season with England in 2001 he was chosen for the Lions tour of Australia and he looks sure to remain a very influential member of the England pack for the foreseeable future.

IAIN BALSHAW

It is hard to believe that Iain Balshaw was virtually unknown two years ago, and yet by the start of this season he had collected 11 caps for England and enjoyed his first Lions tour. Only 21 years of age, he has had a quite meteoric rise, but it has been thoroughly deserved, as he has proved in a very short time that he is unquestionably a special talent. He has that most precious of commodities – searing pace; he is possibly the fastest full back in international rugby at the moment. That is hardly surprising, as he has played most of his senior rugby on the wing for Bath rather than at full back.

Balshaw won his first cap when he came on as a replacement against Ireland in 2000, and four of his next five caps were also all won as a replacement. However, by the end of the 2001 Six Nations Championship he had established himself in the England team as an extremely exciting running full back and he deserved his selection for the Lions. He may lack experience, but he is a player of huge potential.

FRANCE

OLIVIER MAGNE

The French have been very disappointing ever since their heroic and stunning victory over New Zealand in the semi-finals of the World Cup in 1999. They hit the heights that day, but they have plumbed the depths in almost every game since then. Their forwards have lacked consistency and commitment and they have failed to fulfil their potential. Olivier Magne is their one outstanding player and he has remained their one forward of genuine world class. He has the speed and instinct of a great open-side flanker, he reads the game well, he has great hands and he is a tremendous defensive player as well.

However, arguably in this current French side his most important asset is the fact that he is furiously competitive and by leading from the front he must just inspire the rest of his team-mates to raise their game. The best hope for the French is to build their pack around Magne, Fabien Pelous and Raphael Ibanez, because if the forwards do not raise their performance there is very little their talented backs can do.

THOMAS CASTAIGNEDE

The main problem for the French selectors this season will be where to play Thomas Castaignède. They will be the first to admit that they seriously missed their most outstanding back when he was ruled out for the whole season with a serious leg injury last year. For all the skills of their top-class wings – Philippe Bernat-Salles and Christophe Dominici – they lacked the ability in midfield to create the space for the players out wide. That coupled with the fact that full back Jean-Luc Sadourny, at 34, is past his best meant the French looked very ordinary in attack.

A fit-again Thomas Castaignède is exactly the man to ignite the French team. He is a brilliant attacking player, who would probably be at his most effective at either fly half or full back, and it is hoped the selectors will resist the temptation to play him in the centre. What they need is a playmaker at fly half, and that should be Castaignède.

IRELAND

RONAN O'GARA

The Irish have produced a few great fly halves in the last three decades, notably Mike Gibson, Tony Ward and Ollie Campbell, and there is no doubt Ronan O'Gara has the potential to be a key player in the Ireland team for many years to come. He won his first full cap in February 2000 against Scotland in Dublin and by the time he was selected for the Lions this summer he had played 11 times for Ireland. He has scored 152 points in international rugby, including one try along with 27 penalties and 33 conversions. He scored 30 points against Italy and he helped Munster reach the final of the European Cup last year.

O'Gara also established himself in the Ireland side alongside scrum half Peter Stringer, and these two young players could be a very influential pair of half backs over the next three or four years. As can be seen from the fact that he has scored an average of over 14 points per international, he is a reliable goal-kicker.

KEITH WOOD

First capped in 1994 against Australia in Brisbane, Keith Wood is now far and away the most experienced player in the Irish team. He has been the first-choice hooker for the past seven years and for the last two he has been the first choice as captain. An excellent hooker in set-piece play, he is also outstanding in the loose, where his powerful bursts in attack have characterised his play. Apart from his starring role with Ireland, he helped Munster reach the European Cup final in 2000 and he helped Harlequins win the European Shield in 2001.

Wood went as the Test hooker with the Lions to South Africa in 1997 and this summer he was once again chosen as the Test hooker on the Lions tour to Australia. He is doubly important nowadays for Ireland because he is not just their best forward but is also an inspirational captain.

ITALY

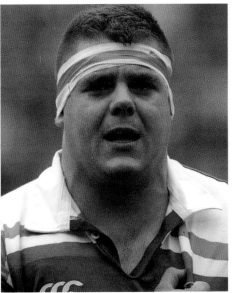

ANDREA LO CICERO

The Italians have had two outstanding forwards during their first two seasons in the Six Nations Championship, and now, potentially at least, they have a third. Their loose forwards – Mauro Bergamasco and Carlo Checchinato – have been as good as any in the championship, and although Checchinato might be coming towards the end of his international career, loose-head prop Andrea Lo Cicero has made a big impression in just 18 months on the international stage. He won his first cap in March 2000 against England, and in his next 11 internationals he managed to score tries against New Zealand and Romania.

Lo Cicero is a good scrummager and a lively performer in open play. Scrummaging has not been a notable strength of Italian rugby in recent seasons, but Italy should now be able to build a scrum around the strength and skill of Lo Cicero. There is little doubt that Bergamasco and Lo Cicero will be the two forwards to carry the flag for Italian rugby in the next two or three seasons, and they are both capable of absorbing the pressure.

CRISTIAN STOICA

The star of the Italian back division for the past decade has been Diego Dominguez, but he is now 35 years of age, and his days in international rugby must be numbered. The new rising star is Cristian Alessandro Stoica, who won his first cap against Ireland in Dublin in 1997 – a match which provided a memorable 37-29 victory for Italy. Stoica also played in the Italian win over Scotland in their first ever match in the Six Nations Championship last year, so he has had little difficulty in adapting to the faster pace of rugby at the highest level. He has played well at full back but is probably at his best in the centre.

Stoica played for Milan at the start of his international career and then switched to Narbonne, where he has been for the past three seasons. This year he has joined Gloucester and he is likely to benefit from playing in the Zurich Premiership. He is a strong, forthright runner in attack and a very good tackler in defence.

SCOTLAND

SIMON TAYLOR

Ten years ago, Scotland could boast the best back row in Europe when Finlay Calder, Derek White and John Jeffrey were at the height of their powers. Despite a run of disappointing results, it looks as if the Scots have the makings of a formidable set of loose forwards once again with the emergence of Simon Taylor, who was aged just 21 when he was selected for the Lions tour to Australia this summer.

In his first season of international rugby Taylor has struck up an impressive rapport with Budge Pountney and Martin Leslie and he was desperately unlucky to be injured in his first game for the Lions against Western Australia in Perth. That injury ended his tour, but he was able to show in that one match that he is a player of huge potential. The Scots are rebuilding their pack, and Simon Taylor looks sure to be a very important player for many years to come.

GREGOR TOWNSEND

It was a huge disappointment to the Scots that not a single back was chosen for the Lions tour to Australia this summer. Such a state of affairs had not occurred on any previous Lions tour in living memory, and it was a pretty strong indictment of Scottish back play. Most worrying of all, it was hard to dispute the selection, although a case could certainly have been made for the inclusion of Gregor Townsend, arguably one of the most incisive attacking runners in European rugby.

A multi-talented individual, Townsend is equally good at fly half or in the centre. He has blistering acceleration and the priceless ability to prise open the best of defences. He was a great success on the Lions tour to South Africa in 1997 and he was unlucky that a bad injury severely restricted his opportunities to impress last season. Without him, Scotland lacked any real cutting edge.

WALES

SCOTT QUINNELL

Still only 29 years of age, Scott Quinnell has already written himself into the Welsh record books by scoring his seventh international try against England last season, eclipsing the previous record of six for a Welsh forward. He is now the second-most-capped No. 8 in the history of Welsh rugby and he is set to overtake Mervyn Davies this season. For the past three years Quinnell has been the cornerstone of the Welsh pack, and he has been the inspiration behind Wales's good record since Graham Henry took over as national coach. He is very powerful on the burst and a good support player in attack and he is also a strong and aggressive defensive player.

Quinnell is now part of a very good set of loose forwards in the Welsh team with Martyn Williams at open-side flanker and Colin Charvis at blind-side flanker. All three were selected for the Lions tour of Australia, and the back row is the strongest unit in the Welsh side. Although Neil Jenkins is the biggest points scorer in the Welsh team, Scott Quinnell is the most influential player.

MARK TAYLOR

After winning four caps for Wales in 1994 and 1995, Mark Taylor dropped out of international rugby for three years. He returned in 1998 and quickly established himself as first-choice centre and a key member of the Welsh midfield. He is a natural footballer, with good hands, an eye for a gap and an excellent defence. He began his international career with Pontypool, but he really developed as a first-class centre when he joined Swansea. He has notched up one or two notable records as well as being named Welsh Player of the Year in 2000.

Taylor has played a remarkable five times against South Africa in his first 15 Tests, these appearances including the memorable 29-19 win over the Springboks in the first match at the Millennium Stadium in 1999. He not only scored the very first try in an international at the Millennium Stadium but he had the distinction of scoring a try in each of his two games as captain of Wales against Samoa and the USA. He deserved his selection for the Lions tour to Australia and he is now one of the top centres in Europe.

FIXTURES 2001-02

* Denotes combined Celtic League &
Welsh/Scottish League matches

AUGUST 2001

Sat, 18th Celtic League (1)
Welsh/Scottish League (1)*
Middlesex Charity Sevens
(Twickenham)
Sat, 25th Senior Cup (Qual Rd) England
Celtic League (2)
Welsh/Scottish League (2)*
Scottish National (Sc Nat) 2 (1)
Tue, 28th &
Wed, 29th Celtic League (3), including
Munster v Connacht (Irish I-P)
Welsh/Scottish League (3)*
Fri, 31st Leinster v Ulster (Irish I-P & CL)

SEPTEMBER 2001

Sat, 1st Zurich Prem Lge (1)
English Nat Lge 1, 2, 3N/S (1)
Senior Cup (Prelim Rd) England
Celtic League (4)
Scottish Prem 1-3 (1)
Sc Nat 1/3, 4, 5N/W/E/M (1)
Scottish National 2 (2)
Welsh/Scottish League (4)*
Welsh Lge 1, 2, 3E/W (1)
Welsh Principality Cup (Prelim Rd)
Sat, 8th Zurich Prem Lge (2)
English Nat Lge 1, 2, 3N/S (2)
English Nat 12 Team Lgs (1)
Celtic League (5)
BT Cellnet Cups (Rd 1) Scotland
Scottish Prem 1-3 (2)
Welsh Principality Cup (Rd 1)
Welsh/Scottish League (5)*
Welsh Lge 1, 2, 3E/W (2)
Tue, 11th &
Wed, 12th Celtic League (6)
Scottish National 2 (3)
Welsh/Scottish League (6)*
Welsh Lge 1 (3)
Sat, 15th Zurich Prem Lge (3)
English Nat Lge 1, 2 (3)
Senior Cup (Rd 1) England
I'mediate Cup (Rd 1) England
Junior Cup (Rd 1) England
Celtic League (7)
Scottish Prem 1-3 (3)
Sc Nat 1/3, 4, 5N/W/E/M (2)
Scottish National 2 (4)
Welsh/Scottish League (7)*
Welsh Lge 1 (4); 2, 3E/W (3)

Sat, 22nd SCOTLAND v IRELAND
(2001 6 Nats, Murrayfield)
Zurich Prem Lge (4)
English Nat Lge 1, 2 (4)
English Nat Lge 3N/S (3)
English Nat 12 Team Lgs (2)
English Nat 10 Team Lgs (1)
Welsh Principality Cup (Rd 2)
Welsh/Scottish League (8)
Welsh Lge 1 (5); 2 (4)
Sun, 23rd Scottish Prem 1-3 (4)
Sc Nat 1/3, 4, 5N/W/E/M (3)
Scottish National 2 (5)
Sat, 29th European Cup & Shield (Rd 1)
English Nat Lge 1 (5)
Senior Cup (Rd 2) England
English Nat 12 Team Lgs (3)
English Nat 10 Team Lgs (2)
Scottish Prem 1-3 (5)
Sc Nat 1/3, 4, 5N/W/E/M (4)
Scottish National 2 (6)
Welsh Lge 1 (6); 2 (5); 3E/W (4)
AIB Leagues 1-3 (1) Ireland

OCTOBER 2001

Tue, 2nd Welsh Lge 1 (7)
Sat, 6th European Cup & Shield (Rd 2)
English Nat Lge 1 (6); 2 (5)
English Nat Lge 3N/S (4)
English Nat 12 Team Lgs (4)
English Nat 10 Team Lgs (3)
Scottish Prem 1-3 (6)
Sc Nat 1/3, 4, 5N/W/E/M (5)
Scottish National 2 (7)
Welsh Lge 1 (8); 2 (6); 3E/W (5)
AIB Leagues 1-3 (2) Ireland
Sat, 13th WALES v IRELAND
(2001 6 Nations, Cardiff)
Zurich Prem Lge (5)
Senior Cup (Rd 3) England
I'mediate Cup (Rd 2) England
Junior Cup (Rd 2) England
BT Cellnet Cups (Rd 2) Scotland
Scottish Prem 1-3 (7)
Welsh/Scottish League (9)
Sat, 20th IRELAND v ENGLAND
(2001 6 Nations, Dublin)
Zurich Prem Lge (6)
English Nat Lge 1 (7); 2 (6)
English Nat Lge 3N/S (5)
English Nat 12 Team Lgs (5)
English Nat 10 Team Lgs (4)
Scottish Prem 1-3 (8)
Sc Nat 1/3, 4, 5N/W/E/M (6)

Scottish National 2 (8)
Welsh Principality Cup (Rd 3)
Welsh/Scottish League (10)
Welsh Lge 1 (9)
Sat, 27th European Cup & Shield (Rd 3)
English Nat Lge 1 (8); 2 (7)
English Nat Lge 3N/S (6)
English Nat 12 Team Lgs (6)
English Nat 10 Team Lgs (5)
Scottish Prem 1-3 (9)
Sc Nat 1/3, 4, 5N/W/E/M (7)
Scottish National 2 (9)
Welsh Lge 1 (10); 2 (7); 3E/W (6)
AIB Leagues 1-3 (3) Ireland

NOVEMBER 2001

Sat, 3rd   European Cup & Shield (Rd 4)
English Nat Lge 3N/S (7)
Senior Cup (Rd 4) England
I'mediate Cup (Rd 3) England
Junior Cup (Rd 3) England
BT Cellnet Cups (Rd 3) Scotland
AIB Leagues 1-3 (4) Ireland
Welsh Lge 1 (12); 2 (8); 3E/W (7)
Sat, 10th ENGLAND v AUSTRALIA
(Twickenham)
SCOTLAND v TONGA (M'field)
IRELAND v SAMOA (Dublin)
WALES v ARGENTINA (Cardiff)
Zurich Prem Lge (7)
English Nat Lge 1 (9); 2 (8)
English Nat Lge 3N/S (8)
English Nat 12 Team Lgs (7)
English Nat 10 Team Lgs (6)
Welsh Lge 1 (13); 2 (9); 3E/W (8)
Sun, 11th Scottish Prem 1-3 (10)
Sc Nat 1/3, 4, 5N/W/E/M (8)
Scottish National 2 (10)
Sat, 17th ENGLAND v ROMANIA (T'ham)
IRELAND v NZ (Dublin)
WALES v TONGA (Cardiff)
Zurich Prem Lge (8)
English Nat Lge 1 (10); 2 (9)
English Nat Lge 3N/S (9)
English Nat 12 Team Lgs (8)
English Nat 10 Team Lgs (7)
BT Cellnet Cups (Rd 4) Scotland
Welsh Lge 1 (14); 2 (10)
Welsh Lge 3E/W (9)
Sun, 18th SCOTLAND v CANADA
(Murrayfield)
Wed, 21st Cbd Services v Barbarians
Sat, 24th ENGLAND v SA (T'ham)
SCOTLAND v NZ (M'field)
IRELAND v CANADA (Dublin)
Zurich Prem Lge (9)
English Nat Lge 2, 3N/S (10)
Senior Cup (Rd 5) England
I'mediate Cup (Rd 4) England

Junior Cup (Rd 4) England
Welsh Principality Cup (Rd 4)
Welsh Lge 1 (15)
Sun, 25th WALES v AUSTRALIA (Cardiff)
Scottish National 2 (11)
Tue, 27th/
Wed, 28th Welsh Lge 1 (16)
Wed, 28th Barbarians v Australia (prov)

DECEMBER 2001

Sat, 1st   Zurich Prem Lge (10)
English Nat Lge 1, 2, 3N/S (11)
English Nat 12 Team Lgs (9)
English Nat 10 Team Lgs (8)
Celtic League (Quarter-finals)
Scottish Prem 1-3 (11)
Sc Nat 1/3, 4, 5N/W/E/M (9)
Scottish National 2 (12)
Welsh Lge 1 (17); 2 (11)
Welsh Lge 3E/W (10)
AIB Leagues 1-3 (5) Ireland
Tue, 4th &
Wed, 5th   Zurich Prem Lge (11)
Sat, 8th   Zurich Prem Lge (12)
English Nat Lge 1, 2, 3N/S (12)
English Nat 12 Team Lgs (10)
English Nat 10 Team Lgs (9)
Celtic League (Semi-finals)
BT Cellnet Cups (Rd 5) Scotland
Welsh/Scottish League (11)
Welsh Lge 1 (18); 2 (12)
Welsh Lge 3E/W (11)
AIB Leagues 1-3 (6) Ireland
Tue, 11th Varsity Match; University U21
Match (both T'ham)
Sat, 15th English Nat Lge 2, 3N/S (13)
Senior Cup (Rd 6) England
I'mediate Cup (Rd 5) England
Junior Cup (Rd 5) England
Celtic League Final
Scottish Prem 1-3 (12)
Sc Nat 1/3, 4, 5N/W/E/M (10)
Scottish National 2 (13)
Welsh/Scottish League (12)
Welsh Lge 1 (19); 2 (13)
Welsh Lge 3E/W (12)
AIB Leagues 1-3 (7) Ireland
Sat, 22nd Zurich Prem Lge (13)
English Nat Lge 1 (13)
English Nat Lge 2, 3N/S (14)
English Nat 12 Team Lgs (11)
English Nat 10 Team Lgs (10)
Scottish National 2 (14)
Welsh Principality Cup (Rd 5)
Welsh/Scottish League (13)
Wed, 26th Welsh/Scottish League (14)
Welsh Lge 1 (20)
Fri, 28th &
Sat 29th   Ulster v Munster (Irish I-P)

        Connacht v Leinster (Irish I-P)
Sat, 29th   Zurich Prem Lge (14)
        English Nat Lge 1 (14)
        Welsh/Scottish League (15)
        Welsh Lge 1 (21); 2 (14)
        Welsh Lge 3E/W (13)

JANUARY 2002
Sat, 5th   European Cup & Shield (Rd 5)
        English Nat Lge 1, 2, 3N/S (15)
        English Nat 12 Team Lgs (12)
        Sc Nat 1/3, 4, 5N/W (11)
        Scottish National 2 (15)
        Welsh Lge 1 (22); 2 (15)
        Welsh Lge 3E/W (14)
        AIB Leagues 1-3 (8) Ireland
Wed, 9th   Welsh Lge 1 (23)
Sat, 12th   European Cup & Shield (Rd 6)
        English Nat Lge 1, 2, 3N/S (16)
        English Nat 12 Team Lgs (13)
        English Nat 10 Team Lgs (11)
        Scottish Prem 1-3 (13)
        Sc Nat 1/3, 4, 5/W (12)
        Scottish National 2 (16)
        Welsh Lge 1 (24); 2 (16)
        Welsh Lge 3E/W (15)
        AIB Leagues 1-3 (9) Ireland
Fri, 18th &
Sat, 19th   Connacht v Ulster (Irish I-P)
        Munster v Leinster (Irish I-P)
Sat, 19th   Senior Cup (QF) England
        English Nat Lge 1, 2, 3N/S (17)
        I'mediate Cup (Rd 6) England
        Junior Cup (Rd 6) England
        Scottish Prem 1-3 (14)
        Sc Nat 1/3, 4, 5N/W (13)
        Scottish National 2 (17)
        Welsh Principality Cup (Rd 6)
        Welsh/Scottish League (16)
        Welsh Lge 3E/W (16)
        AIB Leagues 1-3 (10) Ireland
Sat, 26th   European Cup & Shield (QF)
        English Nat Lge 1, 2, 3N/S (18)
        English Nat 12 Team Lgs (14)
        English Nat 10 Team Lgs (12)
        Scottish Prem 1-3 (15)
        Sc Nat 1/3, 4, 5/W (14)
        Scottish National 2 (18)
        Welsh Lge 1 (25)
        Welsh Lge 2, 3E/W (17)

FEBRUARY 2001
Fri, 1st   Scotland 'A' v England 'A'
        Scotland U21 v England U21
        France 'A' v Italy 'A'
        France U21 v Italy U21
Sat, 2nd   SCOTLAND v ENGLAND
        (Calcutta Cup, Murrayfield)
        FRANCE v ITALY (Paris)

        Ireland 'A' v Wales A'
        Ireland U21 v Wales U21
        English Nat Lge 1, 2, 3N/S (19)
        English Nat 12 Team Lgs (15)
        English Nat 10 Team Lgs (13)
        U20 C'ship starts – England
Sun, 3rd   IRELAND v FRANCE (Dublin)
Sat, 9th   Zurich Prem Lge (15)
        English Nat Lge 1, 2, 3N/S (20)
        I'mediate Cup (QF) England
        Junior Cup (QF) England
        English Nat 12 Team Lgs (16)
        BT Cellnet Cups (QF) Scotland
        Sc Nat 1/3, 4, 5N/W (15)
        Scottish National 2 (19)
        Welsh/Scottish League (17)
        Welsh Lge 1 (26)
        Welsh Lge 2, 3E/W (18)
        AIB Leagues 1-3 (11) Ireland
Fri, 15th   England 'A' v Ireland 'A'
        England U21 v Ireland U21
        Italy 'A' v Scotland 'A'
        Italy U21 v Scotland U21
        Wales 'A' v France 'A'
        Wales U21 v France U21
Sat, 16th   ENGLAND v IRELAND (T'ham)
        ITALY v SCOTLAND (Rome)
        WALES v FRANCE (Cardiff)
Sat, 23rd   Zurich Prem Lge (16)
        English Nat Lge 1, 2, 3N/S (21)
        English Nat 12 Team Lgs (17)
        English Nat 10 Team Lgs (14)
        Scottish Prem 1-3 (16)
        Sc Nat 1/3, 4, 5N/W (16)
        Scottish National 2 (20)
        Welsh Principality Cup (Rd 7)
        Welsh Lge 2, 3E/W (19)
        AIB Leagues 1-3 (12) Ireland

MARCH 2002
Fri, 1st   France 'A' v England 'A'
        France U21 v England U21
        Ireland 'A' v Scotland 'A'
        Ireland U21 v Scotland U21
        Wales 'A' v Italy 'A'
        Wales U21 v Italy U21
Sat, 2nd   FRANCE v ENGLAND (Paris)
        IRELAND v SCOTLAND (Dublin)
        WALES v ITALY (Cardiff)
Sat, 9th   Zurich Prem Lge (17)
        English Nat Lge 1, 2, 3N/S (22)
        RFU Cup (SF) England
        Senior Cup (SF) England
        I'mediate Cup (SF) England
        Junior Cup (SF) England
        English Nat 12 Team Lgs (19)
        English Nat 10 Team Lgs (15)
        Scottish Prem 1-3 (17)
        Sc Nat 1/3, 4, 5/W (17)

Scottish National 2 (21)
Welsh/Scottish League (18)
Welsh Lge 1 (27)
Welsh Lge 2, 3E/W (20)
AIB Leagues 1-3 (13) Ireland
Sat, 16th Zurich Prem Lge (18)
English Nat Lge 1, 2, 3N/S (23)
English Nat 12 Team Lgs (20)
English Nat 10 Team Lgs (16)
Scottish Prem 1-3 (18)
Sc Nat 1/3, 4, 5N/W (18)
Scottish National 2 (22)
Welsh/Scottish League (19)
Welsh Lge 1 (28)
Welsh Lge 2, 3E/W (21)
AIB Leagues 1-3 (14) Ireland
Fri, 22nd England 'A' v Wales 'A'
England U21 v Wales U21
Ireland 'A' v Wales 'A'
Ireland U21 v Wales U21
Scotland 'A' v France 'A'
Scotland U21 v France U21
Sat, 23rd ENGLAND v WALES (T'ham)
IRELAND v ITALY (Dublin)
SCOTLAND v FRANCE (M'field)
Wed, 27th RN v RAF (Portsmouth)
BUSA Finals (Twickenham)
Sat, 30th BT Cellnet Cups (SF) Scotland
Welsh Principality Cup (QF)
Welsh Lge 1 (29)
Welsh Lge 2, 3E/W (22)
AIB Leagues 1-3 (15) Ireland
Sat, 30th/
Sun, 31st Zurich Prem Lge (19)
English Nat Lge 1, 2, 3N/S (24)

APRIL 2002

Wed, 3rd E Midlands v Barbarians (prov)
Fri, 5th France 'A' v Ireland 'A'
France U21 v Ireland U21
Wales 'A' v Scotland 'A'
Wales U21 v Scotland U21
Sat, 6th FRANCE v IRELAND (Paris)
WALES v SCOTLAND (Cardiff)
Italy 'A' v England 'A'
Italy U21 v England U21
English Nat Lge 1, 2, 3N/S (25)
English Nat 12 Team Lgs (21)
English Nat 10 Team Lgs (17)
U20 C'ship (QF) England
Sun, 7th ITALY v ENGLAND (Rome)
Wed, 10th RAF v Army (Gloucester)
Sat, 13th Zurich Prem Lge (20)
English Nat Lge 1, 2, 3N/S (26)
English Nat 12 Team Lgs (22)
English Nat 10 Team Lgs (18)
Welsh Principality Cup (SF)
Welsh/Scottish League (20)
Welsh Lge 1 (30)

Welsh Lge 2, 3E/W (23)
Wed, 17th Welsh/Scottish League (21)
Fri, 19th &
Sat, 20th Ulster v Connacht (Irish I-P)
Leinster v Munster (Irish I-P)
Sat, 20th RFU Cup Final
Senior Cup Final
Intermediate Cup Final
Junior Cup Final (all T'ham)
County Shield (Rd 1) England
BT Cellnet Cups Finals
(Murrayfield)
Welsh/Scottish League (22)
Welsh Lge 1 (31)
Welsh Lge 2, 3E/W (24)
Fri, 26th &
Sat, 27th Ulster v Leinster (Irish I-P)
Connacht v Munster (Irish I-P)
Sat, 27th Zurich Prem Lge (21)
County C'ship (Rd 1) England
County Shield (Rd 2) England
U20 Championship SF England
Welsh/Scottish League (23)
Welsh Lge 1 (32)
Welsh Lge 2, 3E/W (25)

MAY 2002

Sat, 4th &
Sun, 5th European Cup & Shield (SF)
Sat, 4th RN v Army (Twickenham)
County C'ship (QF) England
County Shield (Rd 3) England
Welsh/Scottish League (24)
Welsh Lge 1 (33)
Welsh Lge 2, 3E/W (26)
Wed, 8th Welsh/Scottish League (25)
Sat, 11th Zurich Prem Lge (22)
County C'ship (SF) England
County Shield (SF) England
Welsh Lge 1 (34)
Welsh/Scottish League (26)
Fri, 17th Edinburgh R v Glasgow C
(Welsh/Scottish League 27)
Fri, 17th &
Sat, 18th Leinster v Connacht (Irish I-P)
Munster v Ulster (Irish I-P)
Sat, 18th Welsh Principality Cup Final
(Cardiff)
Sat, 25th &
Sun, 26th IRB Sevens (Twickenham)
Zurich Championship (SF)
County C'ship Final; County
Shield Final (both T'ham)
U20 C'ship Final England

JUNE 2002

Sat, 1st &
Sun, 2nd European Cup & Shield Finals
Sat, 8th Zurich C'ship Final (T'ham)

Note: The Barbarians will play three fixtures – at least two of them against international opposition – during the latter stages of May 2002.

Mission Statement

The Wooden Spoon Society aims to enhance the quality
and prospect of life for children and young persons in the
United Kingdom who are presently disadvantaged either
physically, mentally or socially

Charity Registration No: 326691